What they're saying about *The Toxic Congregation:*

"*The Toxic Congregation* is a well-balanced book that is not only straightforward about the evils that can lurk in congregations but also what it takes to deal with them."
— Kenneth C. Haugk, Executive Director of Stephen Ministries

"Once again Rediger strikes at the heart of the church's problems—from clergy killers to toxicity. However, he offers a sign of hope through the law of goodness that fills healthy congregations who can bless others."
—Abigail Rian Evans, Princeton Theological Seminary

"Ministry to the soul of a congregation requires big-picture thinking, foundational theory, and personal wellness. Lloyd Rediger's *The Toxic Congregation* gives us this and more. Through the book we can enter into the world of the culture, spirit, and DNA of congregational life. It is food for everyone who seeks to engage the life of an organization."
—Bruce M. Hartung, Concordia Seminary, Saint Louis

"A fresh, highly positive, and inspirational prescription for ways in which congregations (and other volunteer organizations) can become and stay healthy. This book is a *must* read for all congregational leaders—not just clergy."
—Donald H. Fagerberg, Founder and President of Ministry Mentors in Glenview, Illinois

Other Books by G. Lloyd Rediger

Clergy Killers

Ministry & Sexuality

Coping with Clergy Burnout

Fit to Be a Pastor

Lord, Don't Let Me Be Bored!

Beyond the Scandals

The Toxic
Congregation

How to Heal the Soul
of Your Church

G. Lloyd Rediger

Abingdon Press
Nashville

THE TOXIC CONGREGATION
HOW TO HEAL THE SOUL OF YOUR CHURCH

Copyright © 2007 by Abingdon Press

All rights reserved.
No part of this work may be reproduced or transmitted in any form or by any means, electronic or mechanical, including photocopying and recording, or by any information storage or retrieval system, except as may be expressly permitted by the 1976 Copyright Act or in writing from the publisher. Requests for permission should be addressed to Abingdon Press, P.O. Box 801, 201 Eighth Avenue South, Nashville, TN 37202-0801 or permissions@abingdonpress.com.

This book is printed on acid-free paper.

Library of Congress Cataloging-in-Publication Data

Rediger, G. Lloyd
    The toxic congregation : how to heal the soul of your church / G. Lloyd Rediger.
       p. cm.
    Includes bibliographical references (p.) and index.
    ISBN 978-0-687-33224-3 (binding: pbk., adhesive : alk. paper)
    1. Emotional maturity—Religious aspects—Christianity. 2. Religious addiction—Christianity. 3. Pastoral psychology. 4. Pastoral theology. 5. Pastoral counseling. 6. Discipling (Christianity) I. Title.

BV4597.3.R43 2007
253—dc22

                                                                                                         2006029666

All scripture quotations unless noted otherwise are taken from the *New Revised Standard Version of the Bible*, copyright 1989, Division of Christian Education of the National Council of the Churches of Christ in the United States of America. Used by permission. All rights reserved.

Scripture quotations marked RSV are from the *Revised Standard Version of the Bible*, copyright 1946, 1952, 1971 by the Division of Christian Education of the National Council of the Churches of Christ in the United States of America. Used by permission. All rights reserved.

Excerpts on pages 42–43 and appendix B are from G. Lloyd Rediger, *Clergy Killers*. Copyright © 1997 by Westminster John Knox Press. Used by permission.

Figure A on page 72 and appendix A are from G. Lloyd Rediger, *Fit to Be a Pastor*. Copyright © 2000 by Westminster John Knox Press. Used by permission.

07 08 09 10 11 12 13 14 15 16—10 9 8 7 6 5 4 3 2 1
MANUFACTURED IN THE UNITED STATES OF AMERICA

To the Reverend David Clifford Brown, D. Rel.,

one of the finest pastors I have ever known, and

a dear friend

Contents

Contents

Preface

Writing a book is somewhat like planting a garden or crop. Far more goes into it than meets the eye, even at harvesttime: preparations, seeds, water, sunshine, and all sorts of maintenance and care. No wonder harvesttime is such a time of thanksgiving and rejoicing!

I have had more than the usual difficulties while writing this book; it is a year behind the original publication schedule, due to surgeries and rehab periods. So my thanksgiving goes first to those who supported me with prayers, visits, and words of encouragement. Now that I am back to normal, I can see how valuable such support was, and how much I treasure the memories and relationships.

First of all, Vera Marie was ever present in help and caring. Since she is a certified energy massage therapist, her treatments and guidance were enormously helpful in pain management, impairment, depression, and coping, in addition to her professional insights regarding energy management and self-care. I believe more than ever in the healing, nurturing energy this alternative health care system provides, especially when used with understanding medical professionals. Our son and daughter-in-law, and granddaughters joined in the support, as did dear friends Jeanne Maruska (my administrative associate for many years), David Brown, to whom this book is dedicated, professional colleagues, members of our church, and caring neighbors. May God continue to give me opportunities to give the same quality of support to others in their times of pain and impairment.

My deep appreciation is extended to Abingdon Press and Dr. Kathy Armistead, my editor, who graciously extended my contracted writing deadlines.

The interviews, consultations, and conversations I have had with professionals knowledgeable about congregational and pastoral functioning have been highly valued in the formation of this book. I name only a few: Jane Harmes, Kay Huggins, David Brown, Allen McCallum, Dora Martinez, Judy Walls, Jim Collie and ordained members of the Presbytery of Santa Fe, Peter Durkee, David Hollings, and with special appreciation to Sue Gallagher and Ted Pierce, as well as to all those who have given unknown support, or were inadvertently unnamed. All names, locations, and personal information presented in the case studies have been altered for the purpose of confidentiality.

Introduction

Organized religion has long been home to both goodness and evil. We are learning, however, that given the human condition in this postmodern, post-Christian era, we don't get one without the other. This is troubling for those of us who care deeply about the church. We pour our best efforts into research, problem solving, and spiritualized managerial techniques, somewhat like the fable of the blind men trying to describe an elephant they had never seen. And while we obsess about the elephant's tail someone is holding, a voice seems to call us toward the immensely larger issue of the whole elephant and its presence. Perhaps the elephant may serve as a crude simile for the soul. For the soul, or spirit as some prefer, is an immense though often unseen part of the life of an individual or a congregation. The soul of a congregation is a distinctive spiritual presence composed of God's intention and a blend of the intentions of the gathered parishioners. The soul is where primary toxicity or goodness resides.

Though *soul* is a familiar term, it has specialized and dynamic meanings as used here. Attention will be paid to clarifying and applying these meanings to both a congregation's toxicity and its health, as I join others in seeking to identify, heal, and nurture congregational souls.

This is a book about contemporary religious congregations: inspirational ones, healthy ones, dysfunctional ones, and the ones that are toxic. We are all learning, the hard way, that we must pay attention to toxic congregations, for they contaminate, sicken, impair, and may even be deadly. Their hidden costs to denominations are enormous, their abuse of pastors unconscionable, and their collateral damage to the cause of Jesus Christ shameful. Though organized religion has always been home to both good and evil, and shades between, our postmodern, post-Christian era is providing favorable conditions for an expansion of evil.

And though many fine congregations are thriving, many, however, are becoming toxic.

Toxins do their damage without much resistance from the virtual congregations we build in our minds. For our buildings, pastors, and programs still seem to confirm a virtual normalcy. (The terms *virtual* and *normal* will be developed later.) The reality, however, is that many congregations have become toxic—poisonous. And no matter its other possible uses, poison kills.

An Instructive Fable

Reminisce about an ancient fable: A frog and a scorpion are sitting some distance apart on a river bank. Both want to cross the river. The scorpion calls to the frog, "Mr. Frog, I must cross the river but I cannot swim. You swim well. Will you please let me climb on your back as you swim across the river?"

"No way!" shouts the frog, "I know you are a scorpion who kills your prey by stinging them to death."

"Oh, but I promise, I will certainly not sting you if you carry me across the river."

The frog thinks for a while, and feels enough compassion to allow the scorpion to climb on his back. As he swims across the river, the frog suddenly feels a sharp sting. Then slowly his vision fades and his muscles go numb. He calls back to the scorpion on his back, "Why did you sting me? You promised not to." As they both sink into the water, the scorpion replies, "A scorpion has to do what a scorpion has to do."

To describe a religious congregation as toxic or toxigenic may seem to some to suggest an oxymoron at worst, or being irresponsibly judgmental at best. Yet, the term *toxin* and its derivatives are used here as metaphors for *evil* and *sin*. These latter two terms have lost much of their power to describe and warn in this postmodern, post-Christian era. We have neglected the reality and tragedy of uncontrolled evil and intentional sin. Therefore we are unable to describe spiritual warfare and the terrorism of using religious pretensions to foment abusive conflict in congregations and denominations. Further, many are unwilling to recognize that evil is embedded in some religious institutions, and that sin is perpetrated intentionally by some religious leaders.

Purpose of This Book

In this book biochemical and medical terms are used as metaphors to clarify the reality of congregations that abuse their pastors and terrorize parishioners and denominational officials in order to fulfill the agenda of their sin, which usually takes the form of power struggles, vengeance, or entitlement thinking. After presenting cases, stories, and research about religious toxicity, we will talk about what can be done to "cure" or detoxify congregations by eliminating toxins with antidotes and intentionally managing infections (sin) with immunization. We will close with descriptions, examples, and celebrations of spiritual-mental-physical healing and health, all to the glory of God and the spread of salvation, peace, and justice.

"Openings" occur throughout the book to encourage personal reflection and creativity. The openings are places where some details of the cases are not provided, prescriptions are presented and left open for local applications, and some concepts are offered with openings that encourage research and creative development that fit local settings.

While many congregations are toxic, they are not beyond hope or the power of God's grace. It is my hope that you will read this book and find ways to apply God's salvation to bring healing to the soul of your church.

The Love Canal Tragedy

We begin with one of the most informative stories of toxicity, its consequences, and its possible remedies in American history, namely, the Love Canal tragedy. It began with a man named William Love, who envisioned a shipping canal connecting the two branches of the Niagara River above Niagara Falls. He couldn't afford to complete the project, and the partially completed canal area was purchased by the City of Niagara Falls. It seemed like a convenient place for the city and the U.S. Army to dump chemical wastes. In the early 1940s the Hooker Chemical and Plastics Corporation acquired this area and filled the uncompleted canal with its chemical wastes. The site was then closed and back-filled.

Out of sight and out of mind, the issue of the canal seemed closed except for the odors, oozings from the ground, and unexplained sicknesses in children. Since the city was growing, the school system purchased part of this unused land for building a school. But the builders soon discovered the pit of chemicals under the building site and halted construction. The city then constructed sewers and sold plots for low-cost housing, without telling new owners of the dangerous chemicals underground. Soon residents complained of strange odors and substances. In the late 1970s, residents of the area formed a homeowners association to investigate the problems, which by now included a high rate of cancer, birth defects, and seriously ill children. The city and former chemical company owners refused to accept liability.

By this time the media began to publicize news about the contamination, illnesses, and lack of adequate response to the residents. Finally, the U.S. government declared the area a national emergency. Scientists and the EPA documented the dangers. But while the government moved some residents to safe housing, many were left to suffer. Finally the U.S. Congress declared the chemical company liable. All residents were moved to safe housing and a long cleanup began. For years the area was left demolished and abandoned. Today the area is being developed again as part of the renamed city; but, even so, forty years later, tragic consequences remain both seen and unseen.

This story is a metaphor for ignorance associated with the dangers of toxins. These dangers include hiding evidence, denial of responsibility, conspiracy, hypocrisy, frustration, and finally the lifelong consequences for victims, government, and the environment. It is the thesis of this book that this metaphor demonstrates a pattern of denial and abuse of power that is reenacted, in some form, within toxic and dysfunctional congregations. The victims are pastors, parishioners, neighborhoods, denominational offices, organized religion, and would-be rescuers—us.

Even the name of this disaster area—Love Canal—can be construed to be a metaphor for how a beautiful concept (love) can become sullied, or even be transformed into a local cliché for exploitation, conspiracy, and hatred. The man who began the canal left an unfinished mess for others to deal with. Those who dumped the chemicals exploited the regulations and aggrandized the toxic pool. Those who covered it over and sold the resulting property parcels multiplied the hazards. Politicians, CEOs, and lawyers failed to halt the spread of tragedy by denials and legal maneuverings. Even the U.S. government only delayed action, and when it did respond only gave partial assistance. Not until the U.S. government excavated all known toxic soil has the area become guardedly usable. But many of the personal and community consequences remain to inhibit normalcy. This metaphor explains itself, even when applied to a religious congregation. But explanation is not enough; we also need remedies and prevention.

The Love Canal as a metaphor for toxic congregations may seem disproportional or inflammatory, unless we recognize that the tactics used by the various perpetrators are also used in congregations where toxicity reigns.

The Law of Toxicity

We may say there is a Law of Toxicity operating in willfully sinful and evil congregations: Where toxin is intentionally allowed to remain, it will contaminate, sicken, impair, and generate lethal consequences. It will be fatal to God's plan for that congregation. The truth about toxicity in congregations must be stated clearly and passionately in order to break the present tendency of spiritual and denominational leaders to assign a problem-solving pastor to a toxic congregation and then try to get on with business as usual. This tactic ignores the pain and abuse of faithful leaders who cannot manage toxicity alone. And it forfeits effective solutions for real soul care that seeks the soul of the congregation to ad*minister* the prescriptions that will bring healing and health.

The Law of Goodness

We may also note, with hope and thankfulness, that there is a corresponding Law of Goodness present and active in righteous, faithful congregations: **Where goodness is identified and nurtured, the soul of a healthy congregation will bless all it touches.** This simple truth about goodness in a congregation must be stated clearly and passionately in order to break through a prevalent illusion that a healthy soul can stay that way without maintenance and discipline. Health does not just happen. (Note: Issues of toxicity will be discussed in the early part of this book. Healthy congregations, decontamination, and health prescriptions will be featured later.)

Misconduct scandals, devotion to survival rather than justice, and massive disenchantment among laity simply weaken resistance to toxins and the will to eliminate them. For centuries the church has imagined and taught goodness (righteousness), especially here in the United States.

We have paid less attention to evilness, choosing instead to use the more socially acceptable term *sin* (with a small "s"), which seems intuitively more manageable. As long as the church could confine sin to individuals and manage it with ritual and judgment, the larger issues of evil could be dealt with in secret. As a result sin(s) became simply an occasional intrusion in God's good world.

In postmodern Christianity, however, there has been a breakdown of authority; and the social role of the pastor, along with a triumph of business models, has left us without adequate defenses or effective remedies. Scandals and inadequate training have left pastors in a virtual world of trying to be all things to all people, in order to redeem their role. Pastors now find their chief task is to make sure everyone is happy all the time. Spiritual leaders, whether clergy or lay, tend to regard the unmanageable intrusions of evil as breakdowns in the system or as problems to be solved. But evil is bigger than these rationalizations. Leaders who recognize the reality of evil in congregational life now use more realistic terminology for these intrusions, terms such as *abuse*, *battering*, *terrorism*, and *toxicity*. As long as pastors and church leaders fail to face this reality, they will remain depressed and ineffective leaders.

This book will use realistic terms to emphasize the continuing presence of evil in congregations and our vulnerability to its potency.

Toxin

We turn now to a kind of glossary of terms that name the dynamics of contemporary congregational life and that will significantly enlighten this discussion. A more complete glossary follows at the end of the book.

The concept of toxicity in religious congregations became a noticeable phenomenon in the 1970s and 1980s, as diversity, mobility, business models, and the loss of authority for the role of pastor eroded the homogeneity and traditions that formerly stabilized congregations. The church in general began to be more of a reflection of its social and cultural context instead of a leading force. Theological and political conflict and a national sense of entitlement gave behaviorally challenged persons opportunities to attack and disrupt what they didn't like in a congregation, and made the pastor the scapegoat for their discomfort and abuse. Approximately half of American congregations have "fired" a pastor at least once, producing a large proportion of clergy who have been fired and often severely abused. Books on congregational conflict have subsequently proliferated.

It is important to note that the toxins referred to here are often composed of multiple toxic substances, each toxic in itself but more potent in combination. This multiplying effect is recognized in the field of biochemistry, but is less understood in organized religion. We say, "One bad apple spoils the rest," but may fail to take precautions to separate congregational toxins and deal with each appropriately.

Out of my many years as counselor to clergy and consultant to denominational officials, I wrote a book entitled *Clergy Killers* (Westminster John Knox Press, 1997) that has become a religious best seller. It featured the biblical teachings about spiritual warfare. It identified the personal profile and tactics of clergy killers, and offered interventionist methods for dealing with such persons who could not be controlled by traditional polity or by loving accommodation. This book is not a reprise of *Clergy Killers*, for it reaches even further into the mental-spiritual dynamics of a conflicted congregation to find the sick soul of the congregation and the toxic or infected persons who keep it sick, even unto death. Not only does this book clarify the toxicity and dysfunction operative in too many congregations, it analyzes with equal fervor the congregations that stay healthy and those that function so well as to be paradigms for the church at large.

This word *toxin* is not a word common to theological parlance, but it is familiar in this context and more compatible than its reference term, *poison*. It is primarily a medical term applicable to substances that damage the human body and mind. In its technical use it refers to substances generated by living organisms, in contrast to the nonbiological origins of most poisons. In nontechnical usage, however, it is more a metaphor than a material substance. Since we will be discussing toxicity, toxigenic, antitoxin, and toxoid, in metaphorical senses, I hope that toxin and these related terms will be a continual reminder that the contemporary toxins notable in the church can be understood as the deadly and impairing realities now causing so much abuse to pastors, with collateral damage to congregations and denominations.

The Most Common Congregational Toxins

In congregations, the toxins most common and damaging are:

- persistent use of innuendoes
- public and secret attacks on integrity and competence

- intimidation and threats through financial matters
- physical harm (or threat of harm) or property damage
- persistent resistance to programs and ideas unwanted by the perpetrators
- false reports to denominational officials or consultants
- extreme opposition to instruction and orders from authorities
- judgmental actions to the point of theological "cleansing"
- unwillingness to use civil conflict resolution methods
- continual use of disrespect
- violation of moral and spiritual Christian norms

Such behaviors by individuals and groups are our focus. But it should be obvious that toxic intent and behavior, now common in families, neighborhoods, and social environments, are influential on congregational toxicity. These toxins, like biochemical toxins, cannot be dismissed, covered over, ignored, or diluted. They must be identified, treated, and eradicated. This may seem overly severe to some who believe that if we ignore, analyze, or keep trying to negotiate and "love" intransigent control mongers, they will become civil. History and research expose this fallacy.

The Need for a New Vocabulary

As you will note, this book uses several medical terms as metaphors throughout. This is done primarily because our familiar theological terms (sin, evil, transgression, et al.) and mental health terms (personality disorders, impairment, addiction, et al.) have become dulled by disuse or overuse. The words *infection*, *disease*, *prescription*, *immunization*, and *health* are used because they have both familiarity and impact; and because they vividly describe the vulnerabilities, sicknesses, and remedies familiar to us from medicine. However, I will not drop the theological and mental health terminology entirely, because it can still be helpful when used appropriately. In particular, the terms *evil* and *wholeness* and *soul* will be used to emphasize the spiritual realities and dynamics that exist in congregational life.

Goodness

This common and beautiful term has also lost some of its impact in this era of entitlement thinking with its penchant for audacity. Yet, it is a term we dare not abandon or trivialize, for it stands in stark contrast to social toxicity and moral license. The Law of Goodness, mentioned earlier in contrast to the Law of Toxicity, carries a spiritual authority comparable to the Decalogue and the Golden Rule. It states: **Where goodness is identified and nurtured, the soul of a healthy congregational will bless all it touches.**

Using outmoded linear and mechanistic thinking, we could say that goodness is the polar opposite of toxicity (sin and evil). In this quantum age, however, we must expand this duality into a dynamic principle. (Note: Toxicity and goodness have been stated earlier as Laws to give them the highest standing among other terms we will use such as *principle*, *dynamic*, and *guideline*. The static, mechanistic implications of *Law* must be subsumed by the more informative understandings of quantum energy and generativity.)

Let us say by simple definition that *goodness* is not perfection, not a pretension, and not a theoretical construct, nor is it optional in discipleship. Rather, goodness is a dynamic extension of some natural human tendencies toward altruism, compassion, and reverence for life in all its forms. Yet it is also a discipline, empowered by God's grace (Gal 5:22) in that its dependability relies on continual practice and honest evaluation of the consequences of human behavior. We can call it a spiritual discipline such that its intentional practice (Phil 4:8-9) in obedience to God's higher purposes (Isa 55:8-9) becomes an exemplary lifestyle.

In this book goodness is intentionally contrasted with toxicity to help define a scale of reference for the four types of congregations depicted. Though this typology is not fully discrete or exhaustive, it provides the main characteristics that will guide our later prescriptions and immunizations that can lead us toward the dynamics of health.

Congregation

This term once had a familiar, popular, and congenial meaning. No more. Prominent researchers and writers give us some valuable definitions that help identify the past and present meanings of this word. Yet many of these definitions do not include more recent, radically new forms and meanings. Once *congregation* meant a formally organized and governed group of persons who typically gathered in a building appropriate to their needs and mission, with an identifiable, ordained pastor. Though many congregations large and small still fit this description, a growing number do not. Some causes for the change are schisms, secularism, house churches, new evangelism strategies, ecumenism, the emergence of new global understandings of spirituality, and perhaps simplest and most important, diversity and mobility.

Further, we are learning that mechanistic definitions of congregations automatically exclude the nonmaterial and spiritual forms of their existence. Some recognize that there is no generic definition of a religious congregation anymore, except in a virtual world of idealistic fantasy. Yet there are characteristics that are comparable and definitive enough to be useful for the categorizations of this book. In fact it is important as we begin this discussion to draw clear distinctions among each of the four categories we use. We begin this process with some comparisons of representative definitions from historical and contemporary studies. For comparisons we may consider several standard definitions and more contemporary and future-oriented definitions.

The Body of Christ

In Christianity the most prominent and enduring definition comes from the Apostle Paul, "Now you are the body of Christ and individually members of it" (1 Cor 12:27). Here two differing versions can be implied. One is the image and metaphor of a human body, but not just any body, the actual spiritual presence of Jesus in the physical bodies of congregants, that together function as a corporate manifestation of Christ's human body. Here the congregation is the actual physical representation of Christ in the world. Another version simply suggests that the style and functioning of a congregation metaphorically resemble a human body. These images and location of the community of faith are a substantial change from those of the faith community in the Old Testament. Yet the basic concept of an earthly home or meeting place for God derived from Yahweh's request for, and practice of, meeting Israel at a specific location. The high holy places, the Jerusalem Temple and later the widely dispersed synagogues, eventually housed the Torah and became the familiar places of worship and instruction known in Jesus' time.

Where Mass Is Celebrated

In medieval times a congregation was generally defined as existing wherever the Mass was celebrated regularly. Its most prominent location, of course, was the cathedral. During this time laity, as congregants, were largely limited to attending Mass, participating in the ritual, and supporting the charities of the priests and various orders of the church.

Where the Word Is Preached

With the advent of Reformation theology and the empowerment of laity, congregations began to explore modifications in the roles of clergy and the sacraments, strongly influenced by the availability of printed Bibles. Church buildings took whatever form the local environment allowed, with the preacher or pastor being the prime authority and practitioner.

Material and Social Definitions

The medieval and Reformation forms morphed into the now common mainline Protestant and traditional Roman Catholic styles of congregations. The consistency of these two forms, even in our era of congregational transitions, has trained us to define a congregation in material and social terms. Following are several examples.

From James Hopewell we are given a classic scholarly definition: "A congregation is a group that possesses a special name and recognized members who assemble regularly to celebrate a more universally practiced worship, but who communicate with each other sufficiently to develop intrinsic patterns of conduct, outlook, and story" (*Congregation, Stories and Structures* [Philadelphia: Fortress Press, 1987], p. 12).

From Cynthia Woolever and Deborah Bruce: "A congregation is an assembly of people gathered for the purpose of religious worship or teachings. Congregations are voluntary organizations of individuals who join together as a religious community. A *church* is one type of congregation, but congregations also include synagogues, temples, and mosques" (*A Field Guide to U.S. Congregations* [Louisville: Westminster John Knox Press, 2002], p. 83). This definition is from the International Congregational Life Survey initiated in 1999 as a collaborative effort of four countries: Australia, England, New Zealand, and the United States.

From contemporary theology: "A people of God called together and gifted for ministry in a particular place, a people who in assembling week by week weave a fabric of stories and symbols and actions and memories and hopes that endures from generation to generation, and that becomes a finite local culture in which God's promised reign is embodied, if only in moments and glimpses" (Thomas Edward Frank, *The Soul of the Congregation* [Nashville: Abingdon Press, 2000], p. 12). We should note that this idea of weaving a fabric of stories and symbols is also characteristic of much feminist theology.

Congregation: A Working Definition

This last definition is notable in expressing a more spiritual-mental interactive understanding of being a congregation. From "where two or three are gathered in my name" (Matt 18:20), to house churches, moveable congregations, average congregations, megachurchs, to virtual (Internet) congregations, the definition of congregation now must include so many variant possibilities as to make a single definition nearly irrelevant. However, the simple working definition of congregation most applicable in this book is as follows: **A persistent gathering of persons to worship, study relevant themes, minister to human needs, and nurture the emergent soul of this group.**

This book will discuss four different types or categories of congregations. These are:

1. TOXIC—an identifiable group of persons meeting for traditional purposes, but with a dominant pattern of control exercised by a substantial proportion of persons intent upon asserting a prejudiced, divisive, and harmful agenda. The soul of such a congregation will have a thin aura of tradition overlaying a hostile, aggressive matrix.
2. DYSFUNCTIONAL—an identifiable group of persons meeting for purposes resembling some recognizable religious form, but with counterproductive or diverse agendas. The soul of such a congregation will be contorted and unstable.
3. NORMAL—an identifiable group of persons meeting with cohesive and positive agendas, yet impaired by missing resources or leadership inadequate for needed ministries. The soul of such a congregation will have a positive yet blemished or frustrated presence.
4. PARADIGMATIC—an identifiable and inviting group, gathering in open and positive forms, sometimes traditional and sometimes innovative, but consistently achieving worthwhile goals. The soul of such a congregation will have a compellingly positive presence and a behavior pattern appropriate to consensual ministries.

Energy

Energy is the stuff of the universe, the essence of God, "God-ness." This is not typical of the way we normally think of energy. Popular thinking is still tied to the Newtonian (mechanistic) concept of energy as fossil fuel, weather forces, food, nonmaterial vapors, and essences. Yet the quantum sciences (physics, chemistry, mathematics, cosmology, and most forms of biology) are shifting full attention to energy as the source and substance of everything we know, use, and are.

In the past, we toyed with nonmaterial ideas of energy, such as parapsychological forces, ethereal essences, intuition, paranormal experience (meaning anything not explainable by traditional sciences). Yet energy thinking requires us not only to think outside the box but also to think without a box. Time, space, shape, and function are now blended into a perception that all of creation is a dynamic unity of space and time. Energy can neither be created nor destroyed. And though it may change form it remains energy.

We must learn to think of various kinds of energy such as electrical, kinetic, biochemical, heat, sound, and light. Of these, light, according to quantum sciences, is the original and basic form of energy, though some say sound is the original energy. And light exists in two forms, waves and particles. Further, some say that we must rethink our understanding of darkness.

All of this seems esoteric in the extreme as applied to congregations and their souls. But it is my hope that, along with more familiar terms, these concepts will become clearer and will help us understand the omnipresence of energy and the nonmaterial soul that both feeds on it and dispenses it.

In order to keep this radical shift from mechanical to quantum thinking manageable in our minds, we can still think of energy as gasoline for our cars. It makes them go; it must be replenished; and if used carelessly, it is dangerous. And like an automobile, our bodies depend upon fuel (nutrition) in order to live, and we can burn out if nutrition is treated carelessly. Further, a congregation likewise needs energy to make it go. This energy must be replenished; and if congregational energy is used unwisely, serious problems arise. This progression of metaphors (car, body, congregation) leads us more closely to a correct and useful understanding of energy as it becomes the source and content of everything we perceive.

A significant aspect of this dynamic thinking is the recognition that there are force fields within the universe's energy systems. In fact, each of us is a force field that affects other force fields. If we conceive of souls as force fields, their influence becomes more obvious. Further, fractal theory plus holography suggest that each of us—our total being—is a *holon*, a material presence containing all the patterns and coded energy of the universe (see O'Murchu, pp. 42, 52, 56). In quantum terms, we can say that goodness is the positive use of energy, intended to benefit all of creation.

Energy thinking, then, may seem like a radical reaction to the shallowness of institutionalized religion. Yet it becomes viable when Pentecost, the sacraments, the Transfiguration, and the generative presence of the Holy Spirit are taken seriously.

Discerning observation and even common sense intuitions indicate that a congregation in any form follows a key theorem of quantum physics that teaches the whole is greater than the sum of its parts. From this we derive the synergy of togetherness that can be enhanced further by individual and corporate intentions. Intention, conscious or subconscious, is a way to move energy in a particular direction, which is one explanation for the power of individual or corporate prayer. This characteristic of energy also helps us understand why change that comes from inside a congregation is typically more effective than any coming from outside. Consultants and change agents of all kinds are learning to take the soul of a congregation seriously.

The omnipresence of spiritual energy automatically makes any persistent gathering of persons seeking God into a spiritual entity greater than any one member. And since spiritual energy is by definition creative, such a group has spiritual characteristics we can associate with God's presence within any person; namely, it has a soul, creative potentialities, interactive reproduction (ministries), and a nurturing response to being. (Note: The differences between mechanistic or Newtonian conceptions of energy and the quantum physics perspectives will be noted later. And since energy is the stuff of God's creation, it is by definition "spiritual energy." The rest of this book will use the term *energy* and presume its spiritual nature.)

Soul

We speak more readily now of spiritual energy, yet all energy is spiritual. Our souls are energy, derived from God. Energy, as noted earlier, has various forms—this is a characteristic of its generativity, known to us primarily as spiritual presence. Energy is well known in its material forms, such as trees, planets, our bodies. The soul, then, also has various forms. Primarily, there are healthy souls, sick souls, and transitioning souls. In simple terms, a congregation's soul is not a nebulous, shrouded bevy consisting of all the souls of parishioners. Rather, it is a composite spiritual presence that can be felt, nurtured, or contaminated. And it can be notably perceived by the results of its presence.

The biblical references to soul are usually with terms meaning "spirit," "breath," "wind," or even "psyche." The creation stories tell us that the breath of God gave us life, a mandate to cocreate with God, and a soul different in kind (imago Dei) from the rest of creation. And the book of Revelation adds a corporate dimension by speaking to and of the Spirit of the churches.

In organized religion *soul* is a familiar term, although seldom used, except in evangelical circles. Yet it is the pop culture and new spiritual energy movements that are most often bringing this term to our attention again. Even those who use it often seem unable to give the soul rational definition.

Some people see auras and spirit beings, yet their accounts seem satisfying mostly to themselves. We can't look in a mirror and see our own, let alone another person's soul—or can we? Some teach that if we look long enough, know what to look for, and are open to intuitive as well as visual sightings, we may learn about our souls. But the most reliable sensual, material evidence seems to lie in our personal or corporate spiritual history, those times when we feel the Spirit moving to heal or nurture our souls.

It is important to distinguish between feeling good or happy and listening to and sensing our souls. For our spiritual souls are not managed by our autonomic nervous system or mental machinations. A corollary to awareness of soul functioning is becoming conscious of how individual souls of parishioners help define and nurture, or contaminate, the corporate soul. And it follows that the corporate soul has a similar silent yet potent influence on individual souls. One of the methods we will review in later chapters for getting in touch with individual and corporate souls is to take time to write and share stories of life-shaping events and spiritual highs and lows that have standing in our long-term memories, both individual and corporate.

In a brief segue, we can note that business management theory and practice are paying more and more attention to the soul of referenced organizations and corporations. The quantum sciences have helped managers see that there is a real spiritual presence in any human organization. These sciences are much more influential than the old linear and mechanistic theories of management thought. So business consultants (e.g., Margaret Wheatley, *Leadership and the New Science*, esp. pp. 20f. and 85f.) now take terms such as *autopoesis* from quantum physics to identify the spirit of an organization that seems to have a life and will of its own—strong enough to make or break an organization. Walter Wink (*The Powers That Be* [New York: Doubleday, 1998], plus his trilogy on "the Powers") expands the concept of spirit to express the soul of all political, social, and religious institutions. These brief references lend convincing credence to our efforts to identify, heal, and nurture the soul of a congregation. We will return to this concept later.

To understand that a congregation has a soul requires spiritual openness and deep thought. Yet the biblical record, church history, and now business management theory, the social sciences, and energy theory are demonstrating the shallowness of thinking of a congregation in strictly mechanistic terms. The development of quantum sciences and the correlative emergence of energy spirituality now offer a more dynamic and generative depiction of religious congregations.

This book takes note of the soul of a congregation, of a denomination, of individual believers, of observers. In a sense, it's even about the soul of this planet—the universe. But this book is also about cases, patterns, histories, toxic abuse and conflict, stories, trends, traditions, transformations, intentions, and spiritual energy in its various forms.

A congregation's soul doesn't come with instructions for assembly or maintenance. Research can give us a congregation's numbers but can't circumscribe its soul. Theology can give us ideals for a congregation but it does not convey a soul. Systems analysis can provide guidance regarding a congregation's functioning but it cannot analyze its soul. Only regular congregational attendees can generate and tend their church's soul. Yet outsiders may certainly see the presence of a congregation's soul, or experience it through the congregation's influence, ministries, programs, or history. It is my prayer that we may learn how to observe the souls of congregations, assess their health, and celebrate ways to heal and nurture them.

This is not a book about research statistics, systems analyses, or problem-solving slogans. That highly competitive and commercial mix has its value indeed. This, however, is a book that focuses on discerning observations and commonsense reflections concerning spiritual sickness in congregations. But it will also provide realistic prescriptions for healing, immunization, and health.

This is my prayer: that we may learn how to observe the soul of congregations, assess their state of health, and celebrate ways to heal and nurture it.

As a quick exercise, can you describe the soul of your congregation?

Outline of the Book

A brief description of each of the following chapters will provide a perspective on these fresh ways of thinking about congregations—healing them and nurturing them.

Chapter 1 will offer cases of toxic congregations, sufficiently diverse not only to emphasize the variety of truly lethal congregations but also to demonstrate the generic patterns of intentional sin and evil (toxicity) as they are enacted by a portion of the congregation large enough, and intentional enough, to contaminate and control the whole.

A summary of the chapter offers a brief review quiz and hints at the prescriptions and immunizations offered in later chapters for healing, protection of spiritual leaders, and immunizations that may provide long-term protection.

Chapter 2 offers cases of dysfunctional congregations. These are congregations that cannot get their act together. They tend to lack one or more key resources or leadership competencies. The first case concerns a pastor and lay leaders continually at odds with each other. Instead of learning how to meet each other's needs, they blame or make excuses, while resisting outside assistance. Frequently their incompatibilities lead them to mutual abuse and threats of resignations and firings. Such frustrations and ineptitudes keep the congregation from growing and enjoying the experiences of effective worship and ministries.

The second case reveals a dysfunctional pastor who limits the paradigmatic potentials of a congregation by personal incompetence. This leaves a glamorous, happy congregation with random leadership and signs of confused ministries for the foreseeable future.

The third case shows a congregation marked by diversity and unable to develop a protocol for managing competitive and dissatisfied factions in the congregation.

The fourth case is the classic clergy-killer case, cited as the opening case in the book by the same name. It demonstrates the now familiar tactics of one abusive member and several cohorts who intimidate by innuendoes, threats, and power politics to terrorize a congregation and the denominational office into firing a pastor.

Chapter 3 examines congregations that can be considered models of normal congregational functioning, yet have potential for both toxic and paradigmatic development.

The first case celebrates the resilience and quality of lay leadership during several major crises.

The second case follows the internal struggles of a deteriorating downtown congregation as it bemoans its decline, then studies the decline to find ways of renewing its congregational life and appropriate neighborhood ministries.

The third case demonstrates how a wise pastor of a small congregation trains and unites its board to see the damage being done by a controlling treasurer, and the board and pastor work together to relieve this person of this damaging leadership role.

Chapter 4 celebrates congregations so competent and creative in small and large ways that they become models (paradigms) for organized religion.

Case one provides a model of exemplary self-management by a small rural congregation that turns its limited resources into youth and parent ministries that transform a whole township.

Case two follows the growth patterns and remarkable congregational competence and vision of a newly developed congregation, thriving on the stimulation of diversity, dedicated stewardship and creativity, and trained lay leadership. This congregation's health and healing ministries have become paradigmatic.

Case three tells of a heart-of-the-city, tall-steeple congregation that turned downtown deterioration and the condemnation of its elegant church building into an opportunity to work as a team with city officials toward downtown transformation, and that transformed its traditional approach to ministry into a remarkable blend of contemporary programs and ministries.

Chapter 5 responds to a question that is a natural outcome of reading the variety of sick and healthy congregations cited in the previous chapters. "Why People Act Like They Do" is the motivational question so important in accounting for the behaviors of parishioners, especially as they relate to their home congregation. An adaptation of Abraham

Maslow's "Basic Human Needs" hierarchy opens this discussion, for it deals with the three primal human motivations. Following will be a discussion of quantum dynamics relevant to our congregations. This is followed by briefer consideration of emotional intelligence, the multiple mind-brains of the human body, the issue of consciousness and observation, and the recent insights on motivation from brain research. The issue of soul will be folded into, and informed by, this discussion.

Chapter 6 is the prescription and immunization chapter. Here one of the "Instruments of Peace," with a specialized procedure and practice called "Grievance and Suggestion Procedure" (GSP), will be presented, discussed, and applied as a basic health and immunization resource for nearly any congregation. It is being used in congregations across the USA as a basic resource for studying the biblical perspective for managing diversity, and abusive conflict; and yet, it works equally well to establish consensual decisions for congregational creativity.

The later part of this chapter is a list of adjunct "Instruments of Peace" that work well with the GSP. And finally this chapter concludes with a list of immunization procedures that support a congregation and its pastor in sustaining consensus and harmony and developing ways to nurture the soul of the congregation with healing and health.

Chapter 7 will apply the detoxification, healing, and health material to the personal roles and lives of pastors. We will discuss the transforming insights and exercises possible for clergy when the presence of soul is factored into both lifestyle and role. An emphasis will be placed on energy management, intentionality, fresh contemporary spiritual disciplines, and personal support systems (with special emphasis on the mentoring process).

Chapter 8 will focus the insights of preceding cases, prescriptions, and immunizations on the nebulous, but dynamic, core of any congregation, namely its soul. This discussion will include the unfamiliar process of "observing" (seeing with the mind's eye) the metaphysical presence in any human organization that is called soul in this book. From such intuitive and yet tangible learnings we can deduce ways to blend with God's purposes in diagnosing, healing, and then nurturing the corporate soul.

Finally, the insights related to the congregational soul will be applied to our personal souls. We will discuss how to include our individual souls in our development of healthy lifestyles.

For easy reference, there are also an index, selected bibliography, and a set of appendixes.

CHAPTER ONE

The Toxic Congregation

In the introduction the working definition of a congregation features its intentional gathering for multiple purposes. Now as we examine cases, we move up close to specific congregations to observe rather than analyze them. We are looking for each one's "soul-print," the manifestations of its spiritual presence. What difference does it make in the community and in the lives of each parishioner? What meanings does it add to its environment? Further, we observe its soul through the implications of its everyday and historical experiences. We will observe its behavior patterns to learn its deepest intentions. Further still, we will gather clues about how the corporate and individual souls that make up a congregation are nurtured or distorted. Most specifically in this first chapter of cases, we will observe how the gathering process, and its continuing existence as a gathered community of faith, can become toxic.

Observation, as used here, indicates a phenomenological process. For it is more than counting, analyzing, or surmising. The comic baseball philosopher, Yogi Berra, is purported to have said, "You can see a lot by observing." Observation in this sense means seeing into, looking beyond, and feeling behind the obvious until a sense of understanding is derived that clarifies the behavior and intentions of this intentional gathering of parishioners.

This book uses four categories of congregations. They are: toxic, dysfunctional, normal, and paradigmatic. We remember, of course, that each congregation is unique, yet has some characteristics similar to other congregations. Therefore, when we study a particular congregation that has a specific characteristic, we also know, although contexts differ, that characteristic will be found in other congregations.

The term *toxic*, as mentioned earlier, brings with it a medical/chemical understanding. Specifically, *toxic* means "poisonous," "harmful," and "capable of contaminating surrounding environments." However, toxicity also exists as a continuum; that is, the toxin may have thoroughly contaminated its host and environment or it may be present only in a small, isolated amount, with gradations in between. But the toxin itself can be identified and an antidote administered, leaving debilitating effects or a clean environment, or even more likely, something in between. When we extrapolate the medical/chemical model of toxicity to theological/sociological/psychological perspectives, we retain the concept of toxicity while adapting the term to a specific congregational setting.

One of the valuable insights derived from toxic congregations is their inability to see or understand their toxicity and its consequences. They lack self-awareness. In fact they may regard as legitimate and normal what we can see as toxicity. As we will see, though some in the congregation may sense that something is not right about their congregation and its soul, all are willing to forgo any self-doubts, the obvious deficiencies, and even abusive conflict in order to continue satisfying their indulgent lifestyles, or at the very least, the indulgence of powerful people. The soul of such a congregation makes decontamination, healing, and health nearly impossible without radical interventions.

The Case of the Religious Country Club

It was idyllic, if you loved golf, horses, mountains, all the amenities, and compatible neighbors. If you did not, you would not live here long. If you pastored the status church in this community, and enjoyed all these things, it was idyllic. If not, and you wanted to preach the gospel, it was frustrating.

Following World War II thousands of returning GIs generated a massive need for new housing. Some developers produced inexpensive tract housing, while others produced new communities that offered all money could buy. People of means often wanted attractive communities that included facilities for recreation and social interactions. A community with a central country club and golf course, horse stables, and mountain activities, was a natural for many. And along with the country club, most also wanted a church where a homogeneous group of people could gather for familiar religious activities. Such a group of residents became an automatic congregation. They, of course, wanted a facility, a program, a pastor, and parishioners who fit their ideals. "Is there something wrong with that?" they would have answered, if questioned.

Sunnyvale Community Church became such a congregation. At the time of its founding the membership consisted mostly of moneyed, avid golfers, horsemen, and retirees who could afford these luxuries. CEOs, professionals, successful small business owners, and modestly privileged others all enjoyed Sunnyvale. A minority of labor foremen, service personnel who maintained members' homes and necessary local agencies, and single persons looking for available partners were fringe groups in this congregation.

This congregation organized itself in the free-church model, with an elected council to govern its internal affairs. The first pastor this congregation selected handled initial issues diligently. The congregation incorporated with about three hundred members. And since it was built early in the life of this community, it grew with the community. Membership grew to nearly five hundred in four years and they built a modest sanctuary with offices and a social hall.

By this time they were looking for a more attractive pastor. They pressured their present pastor to find a congregation that "fits your style better" and leave quietly. Though surprised and hurt, he complied. The congregational council contacted several pastors whom members suggested, and soon hired a midlife pastor known for building a congregation much like their ideal. This pastor was affable, attractive, articulate, married, and, of course, an avid golfer. Within a few years the congregation crossed the thousand-member mark and built an elegant, contemporary style sanctuary with a matching building for the social hall, offices, and classrooms. The senior pastor also added staff—an organist/music director, a social director, and other support personnel. Still growing, this congregation became the preeminent congregation in the area.

The hiring of a sophisticated social director ("our maître d'") established the basic ethos of the congregation. The two traditional Sunday worship services in a beautiful sanctuary were the highlight of the week, socially. The social director filled the social hall, built parallel to the sanctuary with comfortable chairs, intimate table settings, buffets of hors d'oeuvres, exotic punch, candelabras, and fresh flowers, all kept available throughout the morning. All worship services were identical, with traditional music, simple liturgy, and essay-type sermons.

Wednesday evening was the midweek highlight, with book reviews, bridge tournaments, art classes, and a "Bible Survey" class. Other intermittent special occasions were elaborate funerals for members, occasional glamorous weddings, farewell and welcoming parties, and holiday musical events.

The council established a mission committee to develop charitable projects such as donations to groups providing social services to the "needy poor in our area," such as the YMCA, Salvation Army, youth athletic clubs. They also supported two prominent overseas missionary projects. Over several years this mission committee had suggested a Scouting program, meals-on-wheels, Sunday school classes, and job-training classes in the ethnic parts of the surrounding area. But there were few youth in the congregation and persons of color rarely visited, so such programs became token activities.

After some years of such sublimity, the senior pastor announced his retirement. The congregation showered him with farewells, and the council appointed a pastor-search committee while the associate pastor assumed temporary leadership. This committee determined that they needed an interim pastor and selected one recommended to them. The process of leading the congregation through its separation process and preparing it for a new pastor was not the interim's agenda, however. It was soon apparent that his agenda was to ingratiate himself to the congregation in order to ultimately be appointed as permanent senior pastor. Even when his interim contract was not renewed, he remained in the community, interacting with friends in the congregation.

The pastor-nominating committee, after a nationwide search, selected the sophisticated pastor of a thriving midsized congregation in another state. This seemed like a good match on paper, yet after a brief honeymoon, the new senior pastor began to feel resistance to his challenging sermons about discipleship and his efforts to lead the congregation into community ministries. He saw the continuing interference from the former interim pastor and felt the subversion the retained associate pastor was perpetrating. Though the new senior pastor was highly competent and an avid golfer, he was unable to break into the established inner circles of members who controlled the congregation.

Most members of the congregation were oblivious to early signs of trouble. The associate pastor had formed a close relationship with the social director and convinced her that the new pastor would ruin the congregation's idyllic life. Since she had become a close friend to so many parishioners over the years, her innuendoes quickly generated many fears and imagined grievances. Before the senior pastor had completed his first year, powerful members of the congregation began to come to him saying the search committee had made a bad mistake and he must leave. With the hostility mounting, and no visible supporters, the senior pastor sought advice from a denominational official and a couple local confidants, all of whom advised him to leave. They all had suspected that the associate pastor had wanted the senior pastor position for himself, when the long-tenured pastor left. As the personal attacks grew in intensity and abuse, the senior pastor was devastated. In shock and anguish he resigned.

In the aftermath, this congregation descended into turmoil. Members with integrity became disgusted and left, as did those who were disgruntled and confused. Long-simmering competitions and disagreements produced a self-destructive conflagration. The congregation's attendance dropped precipitously, as once satisfying church activities lost their appeal and friends became enemies. As a result, other local congregations attracted many of their members.

Observations

1. Does the agenda of this congregation seem likely today?
2. What is the toxicity of this congregation?
3. What prescriptions suggest themselves to you?
4. How does this congregation generate and use its energies?
5. Describe the soul of this congregation.

Perspective

This case may seem to be a curious one for a beginning to our study of toxicity in a congregation. Instead of pernicious intrigues and blatant abuse, we have an American Dream congregation, with all the rights, privileges, and harmony of a successful church. Any pastor desiring six-figure financial benefits, complimentary country club membership, and low time and energy demands would covet this pastorate. How can we describe this congregation as toxic?

The toxicity is there in maximum proportion from the beginning and with lethal capability. All the picture-postcard attractiveness and harmonious agenda could not save it from a terminal, toxic reaction. For it was designed and maintained solely for self-indulgent persons and families who saw little need for mission and who resisted a gospel of discipleship. When the gospel was preached and the pastor exposed the virtual congregation, there were no internal sources of mental-spiritual health as a basis of healing. The members' only response was an all-out defensive effort to protect their virtual church life. The soul of the congregation had long ago shriveled into a shadowy ghoul.

What is the enormous attraction in such a deadly toxin? Is there an antidote, and if so, what is it?

Antidotes are available that can help such a congregation survive. They are severe, painful, and unlikely to produce health quickly. One antidote for this congregation was the natural attrition of aging, powerful parishioners who died or became invalids. Another was in influx of baby boomers, who wanted an indulgent lifestyle, but who also wanted to see at least some vestiges of spiritual nurture and mission. However, such antidotes did not alleviate the predictable consequences enough to allow health. For the internal competitions, vendettas, and manipulation of financial support sabotaged any vestiges of worship or compassionate interactions. Visitors seldom returned. And the associate pastor who finally became senior pastor seemed to possess few spiritual gifts or professional skills to rebuild this congregation. There were no strong denominational ties capable of producing guidance for decontaminating and building a healthy congregation.

Experienced observers can only dream of engaging a dynamic, visionary, yet wise, pastor who could lead this congregation lovingly yet firmly. The new vision would have to include a community-based agenda with a small, disciplined staff and a realistic plan to remodel the country-club-style building into one conducive to wholeness, community service, and spiritual nurture.

Currently there is talk of such a possibility. Yet the determination of the remaining members to retain the social flavor of this congregation seems likely to prevail for some time. Though affable and sophisticated, these members retain enough control to keep this congregation toxic to any who do not fit their agenda.

Prescriptions for detoxing this congregation will be discussed in the later prescriptive chapters.

The Case of the Virulent Congregation

This denominational congregation of under five hundred members is located in an attractive first-ring set of suburbs surrounding a large metropolitan city. It was established in the middle of the last century as a new church development in a recently incorporated suburban village. It has had twelve pastors (including two interims) since its founding. Its central governing body (the term *board* used here is generic for purposes of confidentiality) has a counterpart in a board of trustees. The board makes governing decisions and the board of trustees makes property and facilities decisions. Annual or specially called meetings of the congregation may discuss or make changes to the decisions or recommendations of the board and trustees. Presently the paid staff consists of two clergy, two part-time professional staff: an education director and a music director. Support staff consists of two part-time employees, a custodian, and several volunteer office helpers. The building facility consists of a sanctuary, fellowship hall, and church offices in the main building, with a classroom addition that was built on about thirty years ago. There is ample parking beside the buildings. All the facilities are adequate but in need of repairs, and the clergy and staff are all underpaid. This congregation has a long history of financial stress, along with frequent clergy and staff turnovers, except for one elderly part-time secretary who has held this position for many years and who essentially runs the staff.

Four extended families dominate the functioning of this congregation. Though not highly visible, they always manage to have at least two of their family members on the governing board, board of trustees, and any significant committees. They called themselves "The Bowlers," because these families are all devoted bowlers. It is common knowledge among parishioners that unless the Bowlers agree, there would be no significant changes from the way this congregation has always done things (à la 1950s–1960s). When they are challenged for their intractable power plays, their standard response is, "We are saving this congregation from secularism by requiring the pastor to preach from the Bible." As one former pastor described the situation, "Secrecy, intimidation, and abuse are their methods." The part-time, long-tenured secretary is this group's eyes and ears. She is their agent in the church office. They have been in control for so many years that the congregation has become enslaved to their methods. Though many members try to be friendly and cooperative, their efforts are lost in a pervasive congregational pessimism.

Another former pastor reports, "I have never been in a congregation where members treated each other so disrespectfully on a regular basis. Since the church facility is attractively located, with easy parking and an adequate family program, new members join frequently, for on the surface this seems like a friendly place to worship. Yet the turnover rate is high because new members sense quickly the negative perspectives and judgmental attitudes. And some learn that even when they volunteer for committee work or run for office, their sincere efforts are thwarted if the Bowlers do not like them or their suggestions."

Yet another former pastor testified that he consistently gave this congregation biblical preaching and teaching, but, just as consistently, received a negative response from the Bowlers and their adherents. "I tried to understand and penetrate their judgmental attitudes, but I could not break through, even with sincere pastoral tolerance and respectful forbearance. I finally gave up for my health and my family's sake."

Other former members and pastors corroborate this congregation's record of abusing pastors. Though this church is attractive in some ways, the negativity contaminates most aspects of its activities. When inevitable clashes occur, such as when the parking lot was repaved, or a new hymnal was suggested, or a pastor was forced to resign, the habit of conflict caused upheavals. Denominational officials are called in on multiple occasions but are unable to generate long-term solutions or peace. Their recommendations and reports are voted down or buried in files. In a couple of examinations of this congregation, an advisory committee from the denominational office advised the board to be more tolerant; to review their mission statement; to pay more attention to their youth; to treat their pastors as spiritual leaders rather than employees; and to bring in a competent consultant to assist them with these needed changes. These reports and recommendations were also voted down or buried in files.

Though the abusive members of this congregation claim frequently that they are keeping the congregation doctrinally pure, they see no sin in the damage they inflict. And since they are willing to fight dirty and rule by intimidation, no person or group has become strong enough to intervene or control them. This is a toxic congregation.

Observations

1. How would you describe the Bowlers' full agenda?
2. What is the toxicity of this congregation?

3. How does this congregation generate and use its energies?
4. What prescriptions suggest themselves to you?
5. Describe the soul of this congregation. How did it get that way?

Perspective

This case presents a scenario familiar to many spiritual leaders. Yet the visible toxic elements are not the whole story of its virulence. Although changing or eliminating the Bowlers seems to be an obvious solution, it is a simplistic response because they control decision making and resources. The common sense and professional prescriptions that seem apparent to observers do not seem so to the Bowlers, who believe their agenda and behavior are legitimate. For long-term members for whom this congregation is home, these conditions have intoxicated them or left them too weakened to effect a healthy change.

The denomination could offer leadership training in the congregation or even send in a prayer- and spiritual-renewal team to conduct healing and revival crusades. Few denominational offices, however, have such resources or the will to use them. Later in our prescriptions we will note effective ways to neutralize, bypass, or perhaps even help remove toxic groups such as the Bowlers.

The Case of North Vs. South Congregation

They don't wear distinctive uniforms, speak different languages, or even live in different parts of town. But they are as different as possible, both theologically and politically. Strange, how they all look like normal Americans, dressing and behaving in similar ways. An observant visitor, however, would likely notice soon that about half of the gathering congregants speak with a southern drawl while the other half speak with a midwestern twang.

This noticeable variation in speaking is more indicative than it might otherwise seem, for this is a congregation born in the days prior to the Civil War and still composed of enough descendants of the North-South divide to establish a natural division in the congregation. That division, though usually spanned by normal congregational gatherings and activities, remains a vengeful segregation in the hearts and minds of many parishioners. These partisans sit on opposite sides of the sanctuary, do not attend events that favor one side, and vote on nearly all congregational issues along what amounts to party lines. The divide is so strong that even members who were not part of earlier struggles feel forced to choose sides in any conflict where these two groups have decided to inflict their judgmental attitudes.

This congregation is located in a small but thriving town that grew in a location ideal for agriculture and related businesses. At its inception, the town was a crossroads of two rural roads. When the railroad came through, a large grain elevator was built beside the railroad. Soon businesses and buildings for support services were built nearby. Houses, schools, churches, stores, and a downtown square and park, where a relocated courthouse was built, became the central area for a town that still prospers. This is an attractive community where people can live and raise families. Yet the residual effects of slavery, civil rights conflicts, and contentious politics remain.

As may be expected, there is deep competition between the two groups. Each side competes for the allegiance of newcomers, seeks favored treatment from the pastor, and fights vindictively when outvoted or bypassed in congregational decisions. Over the years, the church members have tried many of the punishing practices people can use, such as withholding pledges, shunning social contacts with "the enemy," usurping each other's favored parking spaces, mistreating each other's children, spreading misinformation and gossip, and even sabotaging each other's projects and equipment. For example when a well-known musician came to present an inaugural recital on the new organ that was purchased through a bequest from one faction, loyalists from the other side were prominent no-shows.

As with other toxic congregations, this one has enough hospitable interaction going on within each group and in competition for the allegiance of newcomers that an outside observer or newcomer would believe this is a relatively healthy congregation until caught in one of its internecine struggles. One of the bitterest fights occurred over the presence of the American flag in the chancel. The flag would be displayed then taken away, hidden, replaced, and even burned in the parking lot. One Sunday a donnybrook of shouting and fistfights occurred as the worship service began. Both of these latter incidents received front-page coverage in the local newspaper. Abortion, homosexuality, and sex education in the public schools all produced similar hostilities, with picketing of each other's teach-ins and banner defacements.

The pastors of this congregation have been caught in the crossfire, of course. This congregation is part of a denomination that rotates its pastors often, so the conflict and abuse of pastors is somewhat hidden. One of the recent pastors who lasted six years was reported to have said he had to learn what violations of each group's rules for preaching and leadership would be tolerated and which would be punished. A recent pastor told a friend, "I was glad to get out of there alive!" Scolding telephone calls in the middle of the night, public denunciations, complaints about her to the denominational office; harassment of her children, delays in paying her salary, and the spreading of false rumors were regular occurrences. The antics of this congregation would be funny if they weren't so sad.

The denomination has sent in professional consultants on two occasions. One consultant offered recommendations based on a systems analysis of the congregation, which were ignored. The other consultant gave essentially the same report, but claimed he had solved the problems by having the two groups alternate leadership positions on all significant boards and committees. The conflicts continue, as the congregation continues a slow decline in membership, even while adding a few newcomers who comfortably align with one side or the other.

It seems amazing to outsiders that congregations such as this one can continue to exist, but they do. The divisive members become lost in their own self-serving agendas and are too numerous for the usual disciplinary actions to be effective. They continue traditional worship services and programs, but this is a toxic congregation.

Observations

1. What do you believe are the true agendas of these two factions?
2. What is the toxicity of this congregation?
3. How does this congregation generate and use its energies?
4. What antidotes and prescriptions seem helpful?
5. How do you describe this congregation's soul? How did it get that way?

Perspective

This type of toxic congregation is not as rare as it may seem to those who have not pastored, been a member of, or conducted congregational studies in such settings. Congregations such as this one come in all sizes and may have varying issues to defend. But the pattern of control is familiar: generate a loyal power base of persons willing to fight persistently for your agenda; present your views in spiritual and patriotic terminology; learn the weaknesses of those who would oppose you, then exploit them; learn how to stay in control of the decision-making process; use any means necessary to achieve your agenda; never forget that you are right and dissenters are wrong.

To outside observers, detoxification for this congregation may seem possible through attrition, preaching reconciliation, or a mandate from the denominational office. Yet we are learning that historical and entrenched political prejudices combined with theological justifications seldom yield to anything less than radical interventions.

Prescriptions for detoxifying this congregation will be discussed in the later prescriptive chapters.

Summary

In this chapter we have reemphasized the potency of toxic histories, prejudices, and leadership to contaminate, impair, and destroy congregations that purport to be Christian. When the soul of a congregation and its members have become intoxicated, detoxification, healing, and health are only remote possibilities. And those who try to effect remedies are likely to be rejected, infected, or forced out.

Three examples of different forms of toxic contamination help us note the reality of toxic congregations and the deadly consequences they produce, even while appearing to be Christian congregations. The later prescriptive chapters will offer remedies fitted to their needs.

CHAPTER TWO

The Dysfunctional Congregation

Dysfunctional congregations differ from toxic ones in that their deficiencies are more mechanical than poisonous. They may have a tragic flaw that has limited their functioning from their inception. They may have programs or formats that do not achieve desired outcomes. They may have a pattern of incompetent leadership. Or they may have a combination of stultifying location, facilities, or disasters that undermine effectiveness. Unless such a congregation is degenerating from a healthier condition, its typical flaws are not noticed, not remedied, and are defended as part of this congregation's normal functioning.

Dysfunction in a congregation tends to be self-perpetuating. Inadequacies and failures tend to erode morale, resources, and the will to correct dysfunctions and move ahead. Often a dysfunctional congregation suffers from at least a mild and persistent depression. There may well be some good times in which the dysfunctions do not interfere with traditional functioning or when an appropriate celebration brings genuine joy. Even though remedies seem apparent to outsiders, or even perceptive parishioners, excuses, invested limitations, and inadequate resources or facilitators reinforce the dysfunctions.

The soul of a dysfunctional congregation, along with individual souls of members, has a limp or limiting impairment. It does not have a confident presence and may be confused about its limitations. It is somewhat emaciated because it likely is missing some necessary ingredients for spiritual health. And it may suffer from envy of other congregations that are healthy. Since it is not truly healthy, it will be unable to generate adequate energy resources to fulfill its mission. And a portion of its energy will be dissipated in confusion, defensiveness, or in trying to heal itself in inappropriate ways.

The Case of the Heritage That Doesn't Work

This adobe style building is aesthetically pleasing from the outside. Inside, a maze of hallways and dark side rooms feels confusing to those not familiar with the building's add-on floor plan—there are not enough windows, either. The long hallway that passes along the outside of the sanctuary has several niches in which dusty, unused candles wait. At one end of this hallway is a small kitchen beside a large dining-assembly room, where to some the wall colors and decorations may reflect Hispanic tastes. Along the hallway are several small classrooms, one with children's toys, and at the end opposite the assembly room is the Spanish arch entrance to this classroom wing. The pastor's study is tucked in beside the kitchen, opens into the assembly room, and is near a back entrance to the chancel.

The sanctuary features darkened hand-carved pews, while the high ceiling shows its support beam logs in traditional style. The windows are plain stained glass composed of multishades of blue. The aisle carpeting is desert beige. The chancel features a suspended Celtic cross, in the midst of hand-carved communion table, chairs, pulpit, and candelabra. Choir seats are arranged in rows in front of the back wall, on which is painted a mural of a religious procession marching toward a small adobe church within a walled courtyard. An organ shares choir space to one side. A piano stands on the sanctuary level, in front of the chancel.

The neighborhood features a thrift store close beside the church, with a native-arts-and-gifts shop nearby. A very small parking lot completes the block on the other side of the church. The backside of this block is packed tightly with small adobe houses, a small car-repair shop, coffeehouse restaurant, alternative medicines outlet, and sewing materials shop interspersed among the houses of several surrounding blocks. A street dead-ends in front of the church, which once sat in a small plaza. Several blocks away a main thoroughfare carries traffic downtown in this medium-sized city. A very large Roman Catholic parish stands prominently on this main street.

A congregation of about two hundred and twenty-five parishioners needs only one pastor, with volunteers providing support staff. Attendance at worship is about seventy-five at the traditional service, and thirty to forty at the earlier ethnic service. At the first service attendance is largely Hispanic, while at the traditional service attendance is about two to one Anglo. The early midlife pastor is fluent in Spanish, and most teaching and support classes, as well as the Sunday school, are bilingual.

This congregation was founded very early in the twentieth century as part of the hospitals-schools-churches missionary efforts by a major denomination. The earliest pastors were bilingual Hispanics who offered the traditional Protestant ministries, with the addition of Hispanic festivals and hymnody. Though the congregation was formed to serve this mainly Hispanic part of town, Anglos, and now occasionally African American and Asian adults, attend as part of the mission spirit of Hispanics, and because diversity appeals to some members who want to appear to be more like average Americans.

Worship, ministries, and programs are an amalgam of these ethnic traditions, reflecting the congregation's identity confusion. Rather often there are controversies over language, church activities, and teaching materials, resulting in hurt feelings and discord. Such experiences go underground as each ethnic group complains within itself. There is reluctance to air feelings cross-culturally; they are instead expressed passive-aggressively.

Older Hispanic members who have grown up with both the Anglo worship style and teaching materials seem attracted to them, yet want enough of their native activities for comfort. "They don't know whether they want to be Anglo or Hispanic at church," commented one observer. Younger Hispanics sometimes push for more contemporary Hispanic music and activities, but their elders resist. Anglos also are not sure which ethnic style suits them best. The pastor treads lightly trying to please both factions. He tries to stay out of any argument and conflict by maintaining a closed office door and by being away from the church and neighborhood frequently. His ordination and denominational affiliation keep him oriented toward denominational requirements, but limited by non-Anglo expectations. Denominational apportionments are seldom paid and denominational activities are only supported halfheartedly, which causes animosity between the congregation and the denomination. Special

Hispanic activities are funded only by Hispanics. The consequences are a passive-aggressive congregational management style with ministries that lack intentionality and focus.

Newcomers see and feel this tension; and though they may want ethnic diversity, this congregation does not satisfy them. As older members die who remember days when the diversity vision burned brighter, they are not replaced by new visionaries nor interested newcomers.

The congregation dwindles. Recently the pastor managed to offend leaders of both factions, and a joint effort against him resulted in his choleric resignation. A young bilingual pastor has begun his pastorate here with high hopes.

Observations

1. How do you describe the composition of this congregation?
2. Does the mixed agenda of this congregation promise a workable future?
3. What dysfunctions limit the health and potential of this congregation?
4. How does this congregation generate and use its energies?
5. What prescriptions suggest themselves to you?
6. How do you describe the soul of this congregation?

Perspective

Dysfunctions are common in nearly every congregation. Some, however, severely limit healthy possibilities and may even precipitate other dysfunctions. Occasionally a temporary dysfunction is useful for facilitating a superior function, as when a class needs to be temporarily discontinued or moved to an inconvenient location as a new addition to the church is being built. Yet the reason this category of congregations is called dysfunctional is because they have nonadaptive behaviors that seriously limit their ability to function consistently as healthy congregations. These range from absence of competent leaders or leader training programs to persistent unwillingness to support the church's budget at a healthy level; an inept music director who refuses to leave; a long history of bickering and serious conflict; a history of finding reasons to discharge their pastors after only brief stays; a lack of support groups or classes in discipleship in their history or plans; severe environmental limitations; or irreconcilable factions that have existed for many years.

The kind of dysfunctions that concern us most are the ones that impair significant ministries or relationships and that seem likely to become permanent if no corrective action is taken. As in the case above, both the antagonism between ethnic factions and the neglect of helping the Hispanic parishioners find worship and ministry expressions that fulfill their needs combine to generate a long-term dysfunction that keeps this congregation severely impaired. And, inevitably, when the pastor does not please all factions, simmering dissatisfactions and blame are focused on her or him.

The soul of this congregation and its members suffers from high anxiety and continuous frustration. The occasional periods of virtual peace and the ethnic celebrations and seasonal holidays of the church are not adequate to support full spiritual health. Therefore the soul is impaired by chronic pain and unfulfilled expectations.

The Case of the Possessive Pastor

In an idyllic area of the United States, there is what appears to be an ideal midsized congregation that has become dysfunctional. The parishioners are mostly professionals, small-business owners, or individual contractors and supervisors. The staff consists of a senior and associate pastor, part-time education director, organist-music director, administrator, full-time custodian, and numerous volunteer support staff. The building is about thirty years old, well maintained, and adequate for support ministries and creative programs. The budget is met regularly and missions favored by the senior pastor are supported publicly, though the actual money going to such causes is negligible.

The senior pastor has a long tenure as he came to the church five years after it was founded. He often refers to it as "my church." In significant ways it is his congregation, for most of the members joined after he came. Many members comment that, "Our pastor's sermons are what brought me here." He keeps favored members in key leadership roles; and they, of course, support his leadership. Another important factor is his controlling management style. He treats the paid staff as if they were *his* employees. They may not initiate any activity without his permission and disobedience to his directives brings severe public criticism and can lead to forced resignation.

His sermons are intentionally highly entertaining. The biblical content is shallow and he uses catchy slogans to encourage "positive thinking." He uses humor abundantly, along with clever sermon illustrations, film clips, surprise antics and skits, and testimonials from well-known community leaders. He gives public recognition to parishioners for their service. He also maintains a tight grip on the preaching schedule, preaching at all services except when he is on vacation. During those times when he plans to be gone, he requires that the associate pastor submit his sermons for advanced approval.

His weekly schedule consists of being in the church office from ten o'clock till noon, then about two hours late afternoon, except when he officiates at funerals and weddings. The associate pastor is required to be in his church office during regular business hours and has one day off per week. A retired pastor in the congregation makes all sick calls, except when the senior pastor wants to do them. The senior pastor plays golf nearly every day with prominent parishioners or tenured leaders in the congregation. And he is known to attend many movies, from which he quotes in sermons frequently. When there are complaints about "bankers' hours" in the church office, he finds ways to incriminate other staff members. His manner at all church functions is reserved affability. He keeps his private life very private.

Associate pastors do not last long at this church. They either tire of being treated like employees and being publicly criticized or they are forced to leave under duress when they become too successful or prominent. The last associate to leave was asked to take over the experimental contemporary service on Saturday evenings, after the senior pastor found this service not to his liking. The associate pastor had successfully turned this service into a popular one, with much acclaim from parishioners. Shortly thereafter the senior pastor found a way to force a resignation from the associate pastor.

The denomination's officials are unwilling to intervene, since their polity gives much authority to a senior pastor, and because he pays the denominational apportionments faithfully.

Observations

1. Do you have a feel for the soul of this congregation? If so, describe it.
2. The senior pastor has clearly found one of American

Christendom's formulas for successful congregational leadership? Is this all bad?

3. What other persons share responsibility for this congregation's dysfunction?
4. What prescriptions suggest themselves to you?

Perspective

How can such a seemingly healthy congregation be considered dysfunctional? That wouldn't even be a relevant question if this were not also a distressing and frequent operational pattern in congregations across the theological spectrum. Though it is obvious that parishioners are being entertained more than spiritually nurtured, that the leadership model for laity depends on favoritism, and among staff the model is abject obedience, few congregants are now savvy enough to see the malnourished condition of the congregation's soul. And few denominational leaders will interfere as long as there are no complaints from significant leaders and the congregation's apportionments are paid.

To be critical of such congregations, and even term them dysfunctional, may seem like an attempt at theological cleansings, or meddling. Yet, if John 15:1-6 is an accurate rendering of Jesus' metaphor for how his church should function, congregations that produce little outreach mission, that abuse staff, and that provide spiritual junk food for the soul's nurture are indeed dysfunctional.

The Case of the Hidden Dysfunction

This case is a composite of many congregations with which I have worked. It is presented in this chapter on dysfunctional congregations because the highlighted flaw is so common. The reader may note that this scenario could be generated by a myriad of theological-political issues, such as "inclusive language" when reading "sexist" Scripture passages, abortion, peace initiatives, homosexuality, new hymnals or curriculum, and such. A later chapter will feature one of the main prescriptions for healing and health that works well for congregations such as this composite one (see the Grievance-Suggestion Procedure).

The congregation can be any size, in nearly any location, with any functional set of facilities, and with nearly any kind of normal pastoral and lay leadership. The hidden dysfunction is that although this congregation has a denominational polity for guidance and congregational bylaws for governance as required by the state, it has no simple, clear, workable protocol for handling grievances or suggestions for change by parishioners or staff members. The diversity of American congregations tends to trigger ancient prejudices, fears, competitiveness, and an inherent need for one's personal religious beliefs to be the only correct ones. In lieu of mutual-respect reminders as found in John 13:34-35 and Acts 15, behaviorally challenged parishioners forget too easily the pain and disruption generated by judgmental and theological cleansing crusades.

Our composite congregation has a significant and growing number of aging members. Most of them have a long history of faithful attendance with this congregation or a similar one in another part of the United States. Whether they are conscious of it or not, such persons, individually and as a group, feel they have made deep investments in the church, and that their long experience gives them a wisdom about how congregations should function that younger or less experienced members and pastors don't seem to have. Some of them feel a responsibility to issue a complaint when they see things being done or not done in the congregation that appear to them to be a mistake, or at least make them very uncomfortable. Further, many of them have traveled extensively and served in other congregations where ministries and activities that were done seem as if they would be beneficial in their current location. And further still, older parishioners in some congregations are largely ignored as younger persons and ideas seem more "cool" and productive. This makes older persons feel disregarded. All of these conditions can be expected to generate either grievance or suggestions for change, depending on the attitude and experience of the person or persons initiating the complaint or proposal for change.

Most parishioners, including these aging members, have never read the denomination's large book of instructions on how to govern the congregation, nor have they ever seen the congregation's bylaws. Therefore, when they strongly feel a grievance or suggestion for change, they will typically voice these in the way that fits their habit patterns and experience.

For example, a seventy-five-year-old man may be quite unhappy with the initiation of a contemporary worship service now being offered in the time slot in which he and his spouse have always attended the traditional worship service. He and his spouse both tried attending the contemporary service or shifting their attendance pattern to the new time for the traditional service, but find this very uncomfortable and unfair. They begin talking to their same-age friends and find similar discomforts. The more they all talk about this, the more unhappy they become. So this parishioner goes to a friend who serves on the church council and complains vociferously about the disruption and discomfort being caused by this service change. He accuses the council member of not consulting older parishioners about this move and says this unfairness has become a bad pattern in this congregation where the needs of youth and folks with new ideas easily take precedence over the needs and desires of older members.

The council member is caught off guard by this tirade and answers back in anger that it's not his fault that the meeting styles were changed. And if this parishioner doesn't like it, he should go to a congregation where he can get what he wants. This whole episode results in no official action, and no one hears any more about it until this man breaks in on a council meeting with several of his friends, demanding a hearing. The council and pastor try to calm the man and say they will give this complaint some thought, then usher the visitors out of the meeting.

Since nothing changes for several weeks, the man and his friends begin to caucus in the parking lot, over the phone, and with e-mail, until they arrive at a joint conclusion to begin withholding their pledges until the council takes their grievance seriously. With this action the council and pastor begin to look into their denomination's polity and the congregation's bylaws to see how to handle this. Since there is no clear plan of action that covers such matters, they vote to send this man a letter saying the council will continue the present schedule of worship services and that they hope he and his friends can see the wisdom of going along with these changes.

The escalation of emotions, the recriminations, the pain and collateral damage are predictable. Further, the diversity in the congregation and the lack of authoritative respect and diligence in laying out a dependable protocol for handling grievances and suggestions for change leaves the congregation vulnerable to continuing disruption. We can and must do better than this. When the "Instruments of Peace" prescriptions are offered in later chapters, we will see a clear, simple, workable formula in a format suitable for nearly any congregation.

Observations

1. How does your definition of dysfunctional congregations fit this model?
2. What happened to worship and respect for one another in this congregation?
3. How are the energy resources generated and used in such a congregation?
4. Can we truly expect consensus and harmony in such congregations?
5. How do you describe the soul of such a congregation?

Perspective

Some of the congregations we have categorized as dysfunctional in this chapter are like the ones we know or attend. Some readers will have suffered abuse in such communities of faith. The toxic congregations described in the previous chapter are clearly contaminating and deadly. But dysfunctional congregations exist all over the United States, and we seem unaware of their infectiousness, collateral damage, and the financial costs of sustaining them. These congregations lose the spiritual impact they could have if they were healthy.

In the later chapters on prescriptive measures, we will see guidelines and models for dealing with dysfunctional congregations.

The Case of the Clergy Killer

This is the generic case quoted as the first case in the *Clergy Killers* book (see bibliography), and is used here with the permission of Westminster John Knox Press. It is quoted in the exact words that hit the clergy underground of silent, confused sufferers after it was published in *The Clergy Journal* in August 1993. This article was copied thousands of times, and the book has become a religious best seller.

The first signs of the killing process began at a church board meeting. A member of the board, Tim Johnson, said, "A lot of people are complaining about Pastor Enright. They're saying he doesn't call enough; he can't be reached when they want to talk to him; and he's not friendly enough."

Board members asked Johnson to identify "a lot of people," but he refused to name them. Then they asked for specific examples. He refused to be specific. The board said they couldn't take action unless they knew the specific complaints. Johnson replied that they had better take action because these were important members who might leave the church.

In response to Johnson's demand, the board set up an investigative team. At the next board meeting, the team reported that they could find no tangible evidence of any problems. Johnson told them the complaints were real and might have something to do with sexual misconduct and misuse of church funds. The investigative team did some more work and again reported, at a later date, no tangible evidence of such misconduct. Johnson then called for a congregational meeting. This request was denied.

Before the next board meeting, a letter filled with innuendoes against the pastor was mailed to the congregation. At the following meeting, the board and Pastor Enright were in a near panic. Johnson said he had talked to the bishop, and the bishop said these were serious charges that needed to be investigated. At a later date, a new investigative team reported that there seemed to be a lot of people unhappy with the pastor. The board voted to have a delegation meet with the pastor.

The pastor was absent from the next meeting. After months of this harassment, he was in the hospital. The board voted to send a delegation to the bishop and at the following meeting, the delegation reported that the bishop recommended removal of the pastor. By that time, the pastor was scheduled for heart bypass surgery. And it was rumored that his wife had become addicted to tranquilizers.

Observations

1. What is your first impression on reading this story?
2. Cite the steps in the escalation of this abusive conflict.
3. Can you list the strategic mistakes made by each party to the conflict?
4. What is your impression of this congregation?
5. Would this conflict be handled differently in your congregation?

6. How does this congregation generate and use its energy resources?
7. Describe the soul of this congregation (and of key participants).

Perspective

This case has become a classic because it describes in everyday terms an example of spiritual warfare as it occurs in nearly half of mainline and evangelical congregations. The reality of spiritual warfare, evident in the life of Jesus, the Epistles, and the early church has become so repugnant since the Renaissance that we can scarcely admit its presence, much less know and practice spiritual remedies. In dealing with true clergy-killer situations, we learn the hard way that evil does not withhold its consequences when we ignore it ("this too shall pass"), or when we try to negotiate with the perpetrators (can you imagine Jesus negotiating with Satan [Matt 4:1-11] or with the governor and chief priests [Matt 27:11-14]?), or when we expect the pastor to stop the tyranny of parishioners who have given themselves over to the service of evil.

Clergy killers can function vigorously in toxic congregations (note what happened to the pastor who tried to preach the gospel in "The Case of the Religious Country Club") perpetrating evil with little resistance, as well as in this case of a dysfunctional congregational. In the next two chapters we will see that though there may be potential clergy killers, or behaviorally challenged parishioners, the normal and paradigmatic congregations have an agenda of health that precludes the dominance of evil.

This congregation where the clergy killer struck the pastor so viciously, and caused collateral damage to many, was dysfunctional in ways so common that we fail to see them as early warning signals of evil influence. This congregation was an historically notable downtown church, once thriving with religious fervor and mission. Yet in recent years the location became a barrier to easy attendance, many members moved to the suburbs, normal attrition took its toll on stalwart leaders, there was no leadership training program, and all business matters and spiritual nurture depended on the pastor. He was a highly competent, traditional, mainline pastor who had never encountered incarnated evil before. And though the church board and parishioners were essentially kind and privileged people, they were traumatized into inaction by the unthinkable tactics of the clergy killer and a few cohorts.

After much suffering by the pastor and supporters, an intervention was mounted by a vigorous, experienced new pastor, a new denominational official who intervened, and a newly elected board that confronted and controlled the clergy killers. The abused pastor retired to a healthy small congregation that nurtured him and his family back to full health. Many congregations victimized by such uncontrolled evil do not fare as well.

Summary

Four cases illustrate dysfunctional congregations in this chapter. We noted the distortions that developed in a well-intentioned but vulnerable congregation; then the stultifying consequences of a long-term narcissistic pastor; next came an example of a congregation with so many potential conflicts that it could not function healthfully; and finally we reviewed the classic case of a clergy killer who nearly destroyed a fine pastor and traumatized the congregation before a successful intervention.

These cases are presented to show the variety of congregations that exist on the margins of health, and that usually succumb to the impairments of one or more dysfunctions of management, environment, internal disarray, or spiritual incompetence. Such congregations are more numerous than we realize, for we have become accustomed to the presence of impaired and spiritually sick congregations. They are one of the chief causes of decline in spiritual health, lowered levels of outreach and mission, waning membership, and diminishing financial resources of the entire church.

In the later prescriptive chapters, remedies and healthy congregational regimens will be discussed.

CHAPTER THREE

The Normal Congregation

A *normal congregation*, in the common usage of this term, is a congregation that is functioning within the parameters of ministry and governance established by traditional and commonly accepted practice among mainstream (evangelical and progressive) religious denominations. The more focused definition of a normal congregation, as used in this book, is a religious congregation that functions consistently in accordance with its denomination's polity while meeting parishioners' needs and fulfilling its mission at a viable level.

In the two preceding chapters we observed examples of negatively driven congregations, categorizing them as *toxic* or *dysfunctional*. With this chapter we turn to examples of positively driven congregations, categorizing them as *normal* or *paradigmatic*. As stated earlier, these categories have soft boundaries. Though informed by preeminent research studies and compared to popular theoretical systems, these categories are derived from many years of pastoral experience, consulting, observation, and demonstration seminars. The categories are useful primarily for the purpose of assessing dysfunction and health. These assessments then aid in formulating antidotes for toxic congregations and prescriptions for those that are dysfunctional. And they allow us to assess the health of the congregation's and parishioners' souls, thereby guiding the formulation of mental-spiritual nutrition, exercise, and creativity that fulfills God's purposes, and thus sustains healthy souls.

Since the term *normal* is being used in a specialized sense here, a discussion of its traditional and postmodern meanings is useful. Normal, as both a concept and experience, is the driving force in American society and religious congregations. In traditional, common usage, no one wants to be abnormal, no matter what is meant by this word. On the other hand, many people would like to be considered above average (above normal). Yet normal in terms of lifestyle and expectations means being comfortable, which in turn means getting what makes us feel good. Being comfortable, whether this refers to achievements, eating, money, health, or relationships, is our bottom line. Therefore, any call for change requires evaluation in terms of being comfortable before its urgency and value is considered. Normalcy is one of the greatest obstacles to change, whether for individuals, families, or congregations. We want to be comfortable, even though the price and consequences of our comfort is high. When we observe, assess, and minister to congregations, therefore, we must consider the normalcy factor in any evaluation of dysfunction and any prescriptions for change.

As we observe normal congregations in this chapter, we will recognize that they are normal because they want to be, even in the presence of adversity. The souls of these congregations are normal. And since normal works best because of the comfort factor, we celebrate this kind of normalcy because it is good and because it is comfortable for most of the congregation. Yet we need warning that comfort is not our goal, and that one person's (or group's) comfort may cause discomfort for others.

A Case of Consensus

In a small town on the Midwest prairies, a mainstream denomination's historic church building and congregation occupies a place of honor on the edge of downtown. It stands well maintained beside the town park in a largely residential area. The town's Roman Catholic Church across the street was founded in the same year this congregation's building was dedicated. Presently there are about one hundred and twenty members on the rolls, with Sunday worship attendance typically at fifty to sixty persons, including fifteen to twenty young people, besides several infants. In its long history there have only been five pastors, and each of them not only had long tenures but also they were notable leaders in the community where ecumenical relationships are presumed. This is an agricultural area, with family farms still profitable, despite the encroachment of agribusiness buyouts. An implement dealer, auto-truck agency, two grain elevator-feed stores support the farms, while several profitable small businesses enhance the economic well-being.

This congregation has endured hardships and disasters without disruptive conflict. The Great Depression was a time of hardship for the town, but the agricultural base assured survival. There has been some disagreement over relationships with the migrant workers who come to live in marginal housing on nearby farms. The congregation shares leadership in an ecumenical Sunday school for migrant children and tried inviting families to worship and community holiday events, without success.

The new denominational hymnal caused a stir several years ago that threatened to become disruptive until the two informal congregational leaders called for congregational meetings to discuss this. With their respected and competent leadership the church established a consensus to accept the new hymnal. Both of these leaders (a woman who inherited her family's prosperous dairy farm, and a retired government agricultural official) use the word *consensus* frequently in congregational settings. Their respectful leadership reinforces the authority of ordinary citizens who take their election to the congregational council seriously. This combined leadership served well when lightning struck the church steeple and burned most of the roof during the Vietnam War years. Even with continuing disagreements regarding the war, these leaders sought and sustained consensus regarding the remodeling of the building and enduring contrary opinions about the war.

Their leadership wavered dangerously, however, when a rather new but popular young pastor was removed summarily by the denomination for sexual misconduct. It happened midwinter. When the congregation gathered for the Sunday morning worship service, the chairperson of the denomination's judicial council opened the service with an official statement that this pastor had been placed on paid leave, pending an investigation regarding charges of sexual misconduct by an unnamed person. She said the judicial council was following its rules for such situations and would stay in touch with the president of this congregation's council. And she emphasized that for the good of all parties, no one from the congregation should attempt to contact the pastor or his family. Any questions should be addressed to the denominational office, where a decision would be made regarding the pastor and reported to the congregation's council. She also reported that she would handle the worship services for the next two Sundays or until an interim pastor could be brought in.

The congregation was stunned, of course, and immediately engaged in anxious conversations about what had happened and speculations about who was involved. There was a near unanimous outcry directed toward the denomination's chief judicial official and the chief executive official, who tried to reassure callers, but who cited confidentiality as the reason for not providing more detailed information.

The moderator of the congregation's council and the two stalwart leaders went together to the denominational office and demanded that they come to an open meeting of the congregation and discuss the background of this case, options for the future, and guidelines for congregational meetings and programs. Such a meeting was called and quickly became a raucous confusion of anguished questions and accusations. The chairperson of the council gaveled the meeting to order and announced that this was an official meeting of the congregation and would be governed by usual rules of decorum. He asked members of the council to intersperse themselves around the church basement meeting room to indicate solidarity and concern. Then he called on the two stalwarts to speak to the assemblage. They did so with usual competence and compassion. They reminded congregants that they were a local model of the church of Jesus Christ. Therefore their trust was not in a pastor or a denomination but in the God who had placed them in this community to demonstrate forgiveness and faithfulness. And they assured members that the council was staying in close touch with the denominational office where prayerful decisions were being made. Then the council chairperson reported that they had contacted the interim pastor, who had just been named by the denominational office. And this pastor, who was a specialist in sexual misconduct, would meet with them the following Sunday when there would be a potluck lunch after the worship service, with that afternoon being devoted to discussing concerns and options.

That meeting occurred and was successful in calming fears and producing a consensus vote to continue their church ministries under the guidance of the new interim pastor and the council. The congregation recovered its mental-spiritual balance and continues in its consensual model of interaction and governance. And its soul was pleased.

Observations

1. Do you have a mental picture yet of the soul of this congregation as it struggled and functioned normally over the years?

2. What agenda do you believe gave this congregation its internal guidance?
3. What is your evaluation of the leadership process seen here?
4. What practices are models for other congregations?
5. How does this congregation generate and use its energy resources?

Perspective

Being a normal congregation does not depend on size, resources, location, or even pastoral leadership. It depends on the church fulfilling its mission statement and being faithful to God's call to be the body of Christ in a local setting. Recall for a moment the Law of Goodness (as contrasted to the Law of Toxicity) offered in this book's introduction: Where goodness is identified and nurtured, the soul of a healthy congregational will bless all it touches.

The Case of a Mistaken Prediction

Their last pastor had left when he saw that this congregation was not going to fulfill his dreams of becoming once again the dominant downtown congregation in this midsized city. In his frustration he told the congregational council in his last meeting with them that the denominational executive for this region had told him that this congregation was a dying congregation.

After an interim pastor had calmed their anger and fears, she helped them do a community analysis and assessment of their resources. The parish council called a congregational meeting and gave a report on the results of these studies. The report indicated that they were situated in a deteriorating community. They had an aging yet versatile building, with adequate parking, and a large playground beside the church that had once been a source of pride for their Sunday school.

At this congregational meeting, a professor on the faculty of a nearby community college, who was a member of this congregation and had helped do the research for their community analysis, reported that he saw some unique ministry opportunities for this congregation if they were willing to take some risks. He suggested that this congregation could fill a need for a chaplain at the nearby college that had no religious services of any kind. He noted that part of the community analysis showed a significant influx of Asian and African American families who were buying the surrounding houses once occupied by European Americans, who had now fled to the suburbs. Children were overwhelming the city school in the area. Therefore a competent day school was needed and could make good use of their fine playground. Finally, he noted that though there were several ethnic house-church congregations in the surrounding neighborhoods, there was little chance of any of them building churches of their own. This suggested to him that a thoughtful rescheduling of their own congregation's services and meetings could allow a couple of these congregations to rent space from them for services that would meet their needs, at least temporarily.

The congregation heard the reports and suggestions with mixed emotions. Some members said they saw no reason to change what they were doing. Some liked one idea but criticized others. And several prominent members of the congregation reminisced on the illustrious history of this congregation and said they were willing to do whatever it took to have this congregation meet the needs of the community, as they had always done. An insightful member said he thought many of these possibilities seemed possible and certainly fit the model of Jesus Christ, who always went to minister where human needs were the greatest. But what they needed, he said, was a pastor who understood these issues and was experienced in appropriate pastoral skills. Then he made an official motion for another congregational meeting like this one, to continue the discussion.

A longtime member rose to speak to the motion and was reported to have said, "Frankly, what I'm hearing today scares me to death. I can't imagine us letting this fine church die, but I don't yet see how all these new ideas can work. Yet deep in my heart, I feel that maybe God will help us stay here for the very reasons that scare me. I think the professor and our interim pastor have given us some very good material to think about. I second Norman's motion for another congregational meeting. And after we pass this motion, I will move that we all agree to pray like we have never prayed before for God's guidance in these matters." Both motions passed.

A search committee found a pastor who felt called for this specific pastorate. His caring style and patient listening helped open the congregation to the council's selection of a task force to lay out plans for a college chaplaincy, day school, and contacts made to the area house church for possible use of their church facilities. Foundation grants, city government permits, and enthusiastic support from community-minded businesses covered remodeling, promotional activities, and necessary materials. Congregational volunteers were excited about fulfilling service needs. Four years later these ministries are now part of this congregation's normal experiences. Their pastor tells them that they have learned how to transform their congregation's aging soul into a stalwart disciple again.

Observations

1. How do you describe the spiritual process that revitalized the soul of this congregation?
2. How do you describe the leadership in this congregation?
3. How do you think this congregation will function ten years from now?
4. Is this congregation a realistic model for other congregations?
5. How does this congregation generate and use its energy resources?
6. How do you describe the soul of this congregation?

Perspective

This story is being repeated in many congregations seemingly destined to a slow demise and dissolution. Along with the "church plantings," relocating congregations, and remodeling for expansion, congregations such as this one are choosing to become what Diana Butler Bass calls "the practicing congregation" (she has a book of the same name [Alban Institute, 2004]). This congregation makes use of some of the prescriptions to be discussed in later chapters.

When a Pastor and Congregation Become Partners

She doesn't show it but the scars of abusive conflict are there. The congregation engages in enthusiastic ministries and unique celebrations as they enjoy the new additions to their congregational facilities. And the perpetrators of the abusive treatment of the pastor have either left or become supporters of current ministries. This is how a normal congregation should work out its problems and ministries.

When she was called as pastor several years ago, the congregation numbered under two hundred members, had an attractive but inadequate facility, and showed some early signs of coming difficulties. The congregation is a mix of Hispanic and Anglo American parishioners, most of whom live nearby in the scattered, upscale neighborhood of a bedroom village about an hour's drive from a midsized city. She was the first woman pastor, and parishioners welcomed her enthusiastically. The village, which had only three small churches, also took note and paid attention to her presence.

Near the end of the church year, as the congregational council listened quietly to the financial report, among other annual reports, the pastor gently asked if the church financial records had ever been audited. The treasurer exploded with, "How dare you question my honesty! Our financial records have always been in order, due to the careful work of me and my finance committee." The pastor responded that a question concerning audits was always in order, and was not a question about his integrity. The treasurer swept all his papers into his briefcase and stalked out of the meeting.

After his departure, the pastor asked if the council could tell her the cause of this outburst. Their comments indicated that this man had been the church treasurer for many years and had selected his own finance committee. Since the bills were always paid, they could not remember any questions being asked or anyone mentioning an audit. After some discussion, the council agreed that it was time for a reevaluation of the congregation's fiscal policies and structure, and put this on the agenda for the next council meeting.

At the next council meeting the treasurer stood up as soon as the meeting was convened and waved a document in the air. He shouted that this was his resignation from the council but that he was not resigning as congregational treasurer. He shook his finger at the pastor and vowed to tell the congregation what she had forced him to do.

The council accepted the resignation, and after thoughtful discussion appointed a financial task force to study the congregation's financial structure. Then several council members mentioned apologetically that they had several reports that the treasurer had contacted numerous members and criticized the pastor for abusing him and the council for not defending him.

Later, after reviewing the financial task force's report, the council established a new finance committee with a financial secretary and a bookkeeper from outside the congregation. Because the treasurer's term of office had expired, they also had a new treasurer.

The former treasurer sent a letter to the congregation accusing the pastor of forcing him out of office and demanding that she apologize to him in front of the congregation. The letter criticized her for dereliction of pastoral duties, such as not preaching biblical sermons, not being in the church office regularly, not taking communion to shut-ins, and innuendoes about the way she handled money in her previous congregation. He continued his public insults to the pastor whenever he encountered her and wherever there were people around to hear them.

Shortly afterward a longtime Hispanic member of the congregation took up the criticisms, adding her own issues. Accusations about the pastor's ignoring the Hispanic members' needs and issues became the congregation gossip, along with parking lot meetings she instigated. Her criticisms triggered some old feelings of prejudices in this congregation and gained momentum. There were voiced criticisms that the pastor did not use Hispanics in worship services, did not use Spanish-language Bible readings and hymns, and did not support Hispanic festivals. Some Anglo American congregants became defensive, but also criticized the pastor for not keeping peace in the congregation.

The leading Hispanic critic came uninvited into a council meeting and demanded that council evaluate the pastor's handling of pastoral responsibilities by sending a questionnaire to all church members. The council took some time to discuss this and decided that since there had been no evaluation of the pastor and staff since she came, it could be useful and calming to send such a questionnaire. But they selected two respected council members to prepare the questionnaire, which was then sent. At a special congregational meeting for this purpose, the findings of the questionnaire were read. Council members immediately rose to emphasize the positive feedback in the findings. But critics tried to take over the meeting with a crescendo of criticisms leading to a call for her resignation. The council ruled this outburst out of order and closed the meeting with a public vote of confidence from the council supporting the pastor.

By this time the pastor was showing the strain. She began to break down in worship services and asked the council to defend and support her more strongly. They voted to ask the denominational official to come talk with them. The official gave the pastor his personal support and suggested that the council send an official letter to the congregation in support of the pastor. Further, he suggested that the council call the chief critic before the council for reprimand.

The council followed his advice. After she was forbidden to continue the criticisms of the pastor, this woman got up in the next worship service and read a letter filled with criticisms. Then she walked out of the service. The council chairperson then rose and rebutted the criticisms, informing congregants that the council had forbidden any further criticisms from this woman. Then he reported that the council had passed a unanimous resolution in support of the pastor. And further, they were granting her a month of extra time off to recuperate from this ordeal.

The pastor returned refreshed. The council continued to affirm her pastoral ministries. Since then there have been additional Hispanic ministries initiated. Membership has grown. And a new wing has been built to give space for classrooms, a recreation center, and an enlarged social hall featuring Hispanic artwork. The financial vulnerability has been eliminated, their diversity celebrated, and a building addition enhances congregational and community ministries. This is now their new normalcy.

Observations

1. Does the soul of this congregation speak Spanish?
2. What actions and changes demonstrate the health of this congregation?
3. Do you think seminary prepared this pastor for such conflict?
4. What is your evaluation of the denominational executive's participation?
5. How does this congregation generate and use its energy resources?

Perspective

The normalcy of this congregation was not its lack of trouble, but rather the way the congregation and its elected leaders handled various conflicts, and handled with guidance from the pastor. Congregants and visitors continue to express appreciation for the hospitability and enthusiasm with which this congregation provides multiple ministries to this village and beyond.

This pastor made ample and wise use of consultants during the management of the conflicts. And she was diligent in her self-care.

Summary

The three cases presented in this chapter represent a growing proportion of congregations healthy enough to not only adapt to change but also to become innovative in order to meet unmet needs in their congregation and environment.

The historic small-town congregation dealt with traumatic clergy sexual misconduct in healthy ways because they were already healthy. Further they accepted the experienced support and guidance of competent denominational officials and consultants.

The downtown congregation watching its neighborhood deteriorate saw new ministry opportunities and made good use of internal leadership to devise a community restoration in spite of limited resources and the doubts of some. Their pastor supported their efforts and provided appropriate spiritual nurture as this venture developed.

In the small congregation with an excellent environment and growth opportunities, diversity and financial mismanagement were hindering health and further growth. The pastor began to build leadership relationships strong enough to provide healthy authority. She sought guidance from consultants who provided appropriate leadership that freed the soul of this congregation.

There are many congregations that not only sustain healthy worship and congregational interaction but also respond positively to growth and mission opportunities as God's Holy Spirit inspires healthy leaders. Such *normal* congregations provide a counter motif to the proportion of toxic and dysfunctional congregations unable to honor the fresh spiritual possibilities in these days of uncertainty.

The later chapters on prescriptive remedies and the body-mind-spirit health model will discuss ways congregations heal, nurture, and inspire the corporate and individual souls that form the community of faith.

CHAPTER FOUR

The Paradigmatic Congregation

aradigm means "model," not "perfection." The congregations discussed in this chapter stand out because they have a clear understanding of the gospel, are creative in ways that adapt to and lead the social and natural environment, and because they are effective in managing their internal functioning. Further, a careful observation indicates that the soul of this congregation is healthy and likely to stay healthy for the foreseeable future.

Such congregations seldom lead for the sake of leading, nor fall into competition and charm traps. They are effective and paradigmatic for reasons internal and external to the congregation. The internal reasons tend to derive from competent, charismatic leadership, open and energetic members, passionate study groups, and attractive facilities. The external reasons feature effective evangelism or marketing, compatible neighborhoods, and the current attractiveness of megachurches.

We must note with some caution that launching into paradigmatic territory carries a significant risk of losing relational interactions and theological veracity. Such congregations tend to deviate intentionally from standard denominational polity and from traditional practices of piety many still regard as necessary to spiritual and corporate health. The cases and models offered in this chapter suggest that a back-to-the-future approach, the postdenominational megachurch, and the adaptive traditional congregation can all be paradigmatic for a diverse nation.

The Do-It-Yourself Congregation

I heard this charming story from a pastor who was attending one of my seminars. It was during the late afternoon free-time period as I was out doing my daily exercise walk. I was walking the perimeter of a city park near the church hosting our seminar and passed a large tree where a pastor was sitting, leaning quietly against the trunk. He called out to me, so I walked over and sat down. He said, "Remember the story you told of the little girl trying to draw a picture of God in her Sunday school class? Well, I have a story nearly as charming that occurred at a congregation that is about as healthy as any small church I know. A pastor friend who lives near there told it to me."

He proceeded to repeat the story of a second or third grader in Sunday school who was trying to draw a picture of angels. Her teacher had suggested that her students pick a Bible character and just try to draw what they thought that person would have looked like. The pastor then told me some more of the story of this remarkable yet normal congregation.

The teacher of this Sunday school class and her spouse were part-time copastors of a small congregation that could not afford a full-time pastor. Both were ordained but didn't want full-time pastorates, so they shared this one. She had been an arts and music teacher before going to seminary and now was devoting time as a half-day-per-week arts teacher at a couple of grade schools. She also gave some piano lessons in her home. He was in a Ph.D. program in religious studies at a nearby branch of the state university, doing much of his work by computer at home.

The day the little girl tried to draw angels in her Sunday school class, this woman came home and told her husband about it. They both became very excited about possibilities of expanding this class style into a Vacation Bible School program for this church the coming summer. As they shared their developing ideas, they decided to suggest a VBS version of these creative ideas to their congregational council that had decided they could not afford the expenses of a VBS this year. The council quickly became excited about this idea. After the word of this experiment spread around the congregation, several members volunteered to help with planning and other services.

This clergy couple, knowing they would likely have twenty to twenty-five students grades one through six, devised a program that included artwork, music, Bible stories, and some worship service materials. According to age and capability, the groupings had drawing time in which they could draw any Bible person or idea they wanted, but also had assigned drawings, which each student would explain to the others. For music, the groupings could sing familiar songs and then revise or compose new ones. For the Bible stories, the groupings listened to the stories and then added their own ideas of backgrounds and alternative outcomes. The older group was asked to study their congregation's worship liturgy, then write their own versions of the Call to Worship, Confession-Absolution, Lord's Prayer, and Confession of Faith.

Though some conservative members had questions about children trying to write liturgical material, the congregation became excited about doing their own VBS. As the week of actual VBS activities developed, the children and volunteer helpers became more and more enthusiastic about what was happening. By the end of the week parents were so pleased that most of them asked that this event be extended another week. Several said they had told friends from other congregations about this VBS, and they had requested that their children attend for the second week. By then a Pentecostal pastor said children from his congregation could only attend if he could coach his older children with the liturgical material, to which all agreed. The second week was as exciting as the first, with nearly double the attendance. At the close, participating congregations took a freewill offering for the clergy couple.

The council and pastors are revising their normal liturgy now to include some materials the children produced. The small youth group became excited about these ideas and are beginning to write religious words to their favorite rock and rap music, and devise some liturgical materials that fit their needs. The writing and discussing of congregational Statement of Faith, Confession of Faith, and music is now planned to be the basis of training for the confirmation class. Plans are being laid for next year's VBS on a similar model. And a couple of medical professionals are asking if soon the congregations could devise a week of evening classes around health issues, using religious symbols, music, and healing liturgies.

This pastor and I were talking excitedly by this time, as he said he had been thinking about using these ideas in his congregation, even though he expected some members to question them. I had time to share with him a couple of the many stories I know of congregations that retain their heritage while adapting it to postmodern needs and opportunities.

Observations

1. What do you think of the soul of this innovative, paradigmatic congregation looks like?

2. What was the X-Factor (key) in this congregation's move into postmodern Christianity?
3. How did this clergy couple lead this congregation into innovation without inciting criticism and conflict?
4. Does the evangelism and ecumenism that resulted from this innovation seem legitimate and workable for other congregations?
5. How does this congregation generate and use its energy resources?
6. Does the size of the church matter in this example?

Perspective

Our ideas of a paradigmatic congregation now include traditional as well as postmodern versions. These cases indicate some of the vulnerabilities and conflict nearly any attempt at change can precipitate. Yet we have noted that a significant mark of paradigmatic congregations is that they have enough internal health to manage transitions well. It is apparent also that they are grounded enough in healthy spirituality and blessed with disciplined spiritual leadership so that adaptations and innovations blend with God's purposes.

The Tall Steeple Transformation

In the center of downtown a large mainline congregation of a couple thousand members worshipped in an elegant, historic church building with its attached and matching facilities for program and staff offices. Built in the nineteenth century, it grew out of a small but rapidly growing membership of privileged citizens and well-known executives, professionals, and political leaders. For many years it prospered and was known as the most prestigious congregation in this part of the state. Its long-term pastors were notable preachers, and the church board (generic for vestry, councilor session) was careful to engage only the most qualified professionals to lead its music, education, and support ministries. Its stewardship and overseas missions programs were generous and impressive. And its social interactions and community reputation were commendable. They were doing everything right according to all the twentieth-century standards.

After enjoying the great preaching and spiritual leadership of three long-tenured pastors, this congregation's idyllic lifestyle and programs were traumatized by the moral misconduct of the next pastor. Many loyalists could not believe the accusations, even when proved true, and this pastor was defrocked by the denomination. Wiser leaders believed and helped the denomination appoint an experienced interim pastor. This pastor absorbed the anguish, blaming, and confused demands for the return of a previous, beloved senior pastor. Though this was a brief two-year period of serious conflict and vengeance, a strong base of thoughtful, spiritually healthy leaders helped sustain nurturing worship and community service.

Then, the roof caved in, almost literally. The city building inspector found serious deterioration in the structure of the beautiful Gothic-styled sanctuary infrastructure, from roof to lower level. This forced immediate evacuation of all worship and programs that used these parts of the facilities. Again the strong cadre of lay leadership made positive decisions that kept this congregation stable. One of their recommendations to the congregation was to rebuild the sanctuary facilities in a more contemporary mode, as soon as possible. Since they knew that a strong, creative senior pastor was needed to spearhead this effort, their pastor nominating committee searched widely for such a person. They found a midforties, vigorous pastor who had led another congregation into creative growth, and invited him to become their senior pastor. As he began his tenure it was quickly apparent that they got even more than they bargained for. For with their backing, he not only preached a contemporary gospel but also he led by example in the building of strong lay-led teams to handle the multiple tasks of planning and building the new sanctuary, managing a skillful fund-drive, and spearheading the new community ministries he recommended.

The downtown of this city had been in a long decline. The neighborhood around our paradigm congregation was suffering the fate of many such downtown environments. Buildings deteriorated, and damaged streets and infrastructure were not repaired. Parks, museums, entertainment centers, and small businesses sank into disuse or moved to other areas of the city. Open space and abandoned buildings became crime- and drug-infested. Several major corporate headquarters threatened to move, prompting the city council and mayor to begin vigorous rebuilding programs for the downtown. One of the most active leaders was the new senior pastor of our exemplary downtown congregation.

This pastor began meetings with the mayor, city council, service agencies, chamber of commerce, corporate CEOs, business leaders, and financial planners. This combination of leaders generated voting referendums for a master plan and funding. Along with this concomitance, the senior pastor and staff became community advocates. They met with gang leaders, police teams, trash collectors, service agencies, youth and educational leaders, and ethnic advocacy groups. The pastor's well-planned sermons on social justice stirred the somewhat dormant mission spirit of this congregation. Since their building facilities were in the long process of rebuilding, the board voted to buy the U.S. Post Office building next door to the church and remodel it into a central human services facility. A large homeless-persons ministry was begun. The congregation remodeled one of its large meeting rooms into a conference center. They then engaged a talented chef, social director, and electronics specialist to open this facility for corporate, educational, political, and commercial use. This project soon became a center for downtown meetings of all types and generated significant income for the congregation's service ministries.

Community youth programs were headquartered here, along with education programs adjunct to deteriorated neighborhood school classes and activities. The Boy Scout program enhanced its community service programs. Men's and women's service groups set up programs for the aging, impaired, along with support groups for caregivers. Hot lunch programs were set up for all area youth, along with cooperative YMCA programs, tutoring programs, and summer-holiday children and youth activities. The city council, police representatives, school, and religious task forces began to organize ethnic minority interaction groups.

Volunteer and professional leaders began to take pride in participating in their city's transformation. The principal downtown corporate offices made substantial donations, and the city council aggressively searched and found grant monies to fund this ambitious redevelopment. The senior pastor and his lay leaders played a significant part in these developments. This was a crucial part of the transformation of the entire downtown area. As ethnic minorities, homeless, parolees, and mentally impaired persons began to attend—and even join—this once all-Anglo, privileged congregation, the realities of how this massive, cooperative transformation was affecting all facets of the city caused both resistance and negative reverberations as well as wondrous downtown vigor. Yet the continuing face-to-face meetings and positive attitudes of community and church leaders made the transitions work and encouraged everyone to see and participate in the massive changes. The church held celebrations to praise and bless these achievements and encourage continuing efforts. Awards from national organizations, political groups, and religious leaders enhanced community pride. And our paradigmatic congregation began a new phase of growth that included people of color, converted gang leaders, the homeless and impaired, as well as appreciative community leaders who recognized this congregation's central role in this city's transformation.

In a city-congregation transformation of this magnitude, good communications are mandatory. The new senior pastor made a point of regular conversations with the publisher and religion editor of the city newspaper, which had a wide regional readership. Regular news items, editorials, and feature essays appeared in the paper, giving the whole community not only news of the downtown renovations and this congregation's activities, but also wrote of the meanings of such transformation.

It is interesting to note that the several other congregations that had once had a downtown presence, moved to the prospering suburbs. The largest Roman Catholic downtown congregation also stayed downtown, along with the paradigmatic congregation. And though they tried to include the other congregations in the benefits and services of the new downtown, the jealousy of pastors and turf struggles in the suburbs left a negative ecumenical ambience. Yet there are hopeful signs that the continuing efforts at cooperative ministries will generate a more positive attitude.

Observations

1. What do you see as the central dynamics of this extraordinary transformation of congregation and city core?
2. Is it a proper role of a Christian congregation to engage in so much social and secular activity?
3. How can an ordinary congregation learn from and generate such developments in ways appropriate to its environment?
4. Can seminaries and denominational offices train and support such innovative pastors?
5. What are the most important factors in the way this congregation generates and uses its energy, financial, and leadership resources?
6. How do you describe the soul of this congregation?

Perspective

There are many paradigmatic congregations in the United States. Perhaps the most impressive are the ones in which an established congregation achieves such a massive transformation in such positive ways.

We expect megacongregations, if located in fertile environments and led by innovative and spiritually disciplined lay and ordained leaders, to produce the prodigious growth, discipleship, and effective outreach demonstrated by this paradigmatic congregation. The miracle of this tall-steeple congregation is not only its ministries and outreach, but also its ability to facilitate positive community action and internal regeneration.

What had once been a prestigious congregation developed for privileged, Anglo American parishioners became of model of diversity, and social justice, as well as spiritual nurture. The key to its dynamic transformation and impact in the community is extraordinary. Yet the key in its effectiveness is the long tradition of open-minded, and spiritually disciplined lay leadership.

The soul of this congregation is a giant spiritual presence. Wouldn't we all enjoy meeting this godlike soul in material presence? We can.

The Case of the Virtual Congregations

The introduction to this book mentions *virtual congregations*. This term means an act of imagination and vision that takes a convincing and seemingly material form. *Virtual* should not be confused with not being actual, for a virtual entity seems real to those who share the vision of its existence. Some of the benefits of virtuality are similar to those of material existence in real time. And, after all, we all live part of our lives in our imagination (virtuality). Yet what exists only in virtual experience cannot generate the material entities nor its benefits and vulnerabilities without faithfulness from its true believers and participants in its existence.

Trying to examine and derive clear identities and guidelines from the Internet virtual congregation movement is beyond the purview of this book and probably beyond any precise definitions and clear insights. Yet virtual congregations should not be ignored when they exhibit some of the characteristics of normal or paradigmatic churches. A normal or paradigmatic congregation is a church with rapid growth where many nonmembers participate in the life of the church. It is full of passion and energy. Today a significant number of churchgoers also participate in virtuals. Virtuals typically offer support groups, study classes, and mission opportunities.

Virtual congregations are convenient, free, as private as a participant wants, require no commitments, and are often open to theological variation. Persons participate in chat rooms, blogs, and videoconferencing. These congregations usually accept diversity, feature much participant interaction, and have few face-to-face interpersonal relationships.

Yet, virtuals have no membership vows and commitments and no belief requirements. They incorporate much less participation in sacraments and use of traditional symbols. They may offer fewer pastoral services than brick-and-mortar congregations because they typically have no building or facilities for family use, personal identity, or special programming. They also seemingly have little impetus for mission or stewardship.

Even with this limited list of characteristics, it is difficult to see how a virtual congregation can develop a soul, manage spiritual energy, or provide the disciplines important to healing, nurture, and mission. Without a soul (corporate spiritual presence) spiritual health is dependent on the member's own individual soul for spiritual identity, and the congregation forfeits the synergy of the gathered community of faith.

Therefore, even though the virtual congregation appears to have some paradigmatic characteristics and potentials, presently it does not fit this category.

The Case of the Megacongregation

We have included several significantly large membership congregations in our case studies, but none that are presently in the megachurch category (about 5,000 members or more). Again, such congregations do not fit the purview of this book, though most of the megachurches have some of the laudable characteristics of our normal or paradigmatic categories. Their size simply sets them apart in dynamics, potential, and interpersonal synergy.

In comparison with the virtual congregation, the megacongregation clearly has a soul, perhaps a family of souls. Its soul is not only made up of the giant corporate soul but also clusters of smaller aggregates, besides the individual souls of the members. The immense size of a megachurch soul makes its healing, nurture, and individual spiritual disciplines and accountabilities somewhat paradigmatic yet beyond use as a model for the vast majority of mainline congregations.

Observations

1. List characteristics of virtual congregations and mega-congregations you think are Christlike.
2. Which of these characteristics can be useful guides for your congregation?
3. What negative characteristics of these two types seem dangerous to you?
4. How is energy generated and used in both types?
5. How do you describe the soul of a virtual or megacongregation?

Perspective

Though a full discussion of the Internet virtual congregations and megachurches is beyond the purview of this book, such congregations must be noticed and examined so we may learn from their insights and effective ministries. This is being done now, so we may expect the next wave of books about congregations will give us information and studied opinions regarding these two contemporary movements.

Summary

This chapter has focused on two congregations that demonstrate spiritually disciplined innovation as well as the ability to maintain corporate health. The soul of each congregation is healthy, and this gives individual parishioners a base of spiritual energy to keep their own souls healthy. And they then make their healthy contribution to the soul of the congregation. These two congregations are paradigms for all of us because they know how to maintain both internal and external health along with appropriate outreach.

The lessons these two congregations and others like them teach us will show up in the prescriptive chapters where we discuss remedies and nurturing strategies that keep healthy congregations healthy, and provide healing guidelines for those that are not.

CHAPTER FIVE

Why People Act Like They Do

Motivation. The X-Factor. Motivation is the X-Factor, the catalyst, each of us brings to our everyday lives. Much of the rest is a given. Motivation is our intentions demonstrated in our behavior. Motivation begins in the soul, becomes conscious in the brain-mind, and is expressed through the physical self. Understanding this mental-spiritual-physical part of our lives enhances diagnosis, healing, and nurture of congregations and their members. Congregations have this X-Factor also.

Why include human motivation and intention in a book that addresses toxic and dysfunctional factors, and later, the normal and paradigmatic factors in congregations? Good question! Keep asking it, for it helps us open one of the deepest and often hidden causes of difficulties in congregations. We have a tendency to try to solve our congregational problems without addressing the real problem, namely, the inner experiences (motives) and self-management (intentions) that truly drive our congregations and leaders. Devoting a chapter to motivation can help generate some of the best prescriptions and guidelines for spiritual nurture available. Quick example: take a few minutes to go back and read the story of Love Canal in the introduction. It clearly demonstrates the folly of quick fixes, sloganeering, and denial.

Motivation	= generation and use of energy
Intention	= imagined goals, behavior
Attitude	= combining motivation and intention into a mind-set

Motivation is a function of soul; intention is a function of mind. This distinction, although not as clean-cut as language seems to make it, is a valuable indicator of persons who tend to say one thing and do another or who assume a lifestyle for all persons out of their own personal experiences. In their own consciousness this is often not a contradiction. It makes sense to them that everyone else sees the world just as they do. It serves their purpose. They may articulate their intention for effect or manipulation while their behavior is in service to a motivation hidden even from themselves. For example, the parishioner who publicly exclaims, "We need more gospel preaching around here," then after hearing the pastor preach a penetrating sermon from Jesus' parables or Sermon by the Sea, makes a point of criticizing the pastor, instead of applauding the gospel sermon.

We should note in passing that *attitude*, that overworked street word, is often apparent as in a perpetual frown or smile, even a lifestyle. Intention is a focused course of action that guides imminent or potential behavior and influences attitude. For example, planning to stop abusing alcohol but never doing it. Motivation is a need, emotion, idea, or purpose, strong enough and conscious enough to produce behavior. For example wanting to please parents by achieving an A+ on an exam enough to actually do it. Although these two concepts are closely related, they are not the same. It is more difficult to determine intention, since it is often hidden, denied, or camouflaged, while motivation produces compatible action. (Some use terminology such as *drive* or *instinct* to describe motivation and intention. However, I choose to avoid aligning this book will particular ideologies or schools of psychological thought.)

While motivations and intentions warrant entire books to describe, this discussion limits explanation just to issues raised in this book. First, we will consider them in general terms as basic agendas for human behavior, then in terms of general influences, and finally in terms of a contemporary ethics of morality or "Ethics of Consequences."

Since the term *soul* is so important for our discussion, I will restate its meaning. A soul is the spiritual presence of an individual or organization. When related to human and congregational motivation and behavior, it also adds a spiritual, eternal, and God-ness dynamic. The spirituality may be either good or evil; the eternal part refers to its timeless effects; and the God-ness part simply includes the mysterious influence of divine purposes.

Agendas of Human Behavior

The three agendas as discussed here, and diagrammed in "Agendas of Human Behavior," figure A, are influenced by several prominent authorities, such as the Apostle Paul, St. Augustine, Erik Erikson, Gordon Allport, Abraham Maslow, and James Fowler. The intent of the theoretical construct figure A is to simplify some of their teachings and enhance our understanding of the development of motivations and their outward expression. Since it is conceived as applicable to both individuals and organizations, its insights fit both our case studies and prescriptions. The usual disclaimer must be offered here, namely that each individual and organization is unique, thus agenda behavior may vary.

Note from the diagram that the three agendas are arranged in a hierarchical format, with the survival agenda being primary and strongest, the identity agenda next in potency, and the relationship agenda least likely to be dominant. This arrangement immediately offends our Christian ideal, in which we imagine loving relationships are our primary agenda. Yet, when we factor together the body, mind, and spirit, it is apparent the hierarchy is accurate, though it may be modified appropriately. Note also that each agenda has a positive and a negative emotion that governs it. This is significant for our understanding of the flow of energy and how human beings manage this flow. The polarity creates the shifts from negative to positive in thinking and behavior as a person perceives and responds to life's events and opportunities. Please note that negative and positive are not judgmental terms; as used here, they simply identify the polarity and its influence on the flow of energy.

Note further that there is movement between the agendas, sometimes instantaneous, sometime moving slowly as a person responds to life. We can see the dominance of the survival agenda in young children for whom physical needs and comfort trump all other behavioral options until they are satisfied. Yet, as survival needs are met, even a young child is able to move to the next higher agenda.

AGENDAS FOR HUMAN BEHAVIOR

AGENDA   EMOTION FELT

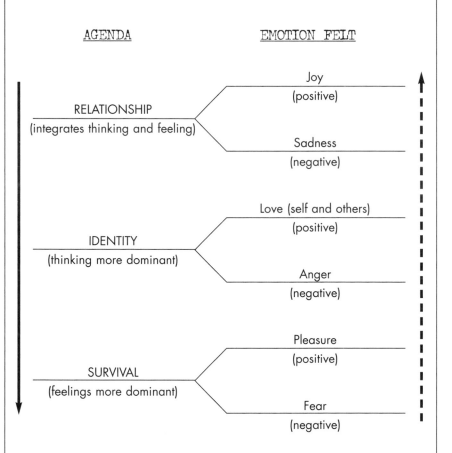

LEGEND
AGENDA = primary, overriding motivation pattern
EMOTION = a set of feelings that induce physiological change and behavior
SOLID ARROW = downward pressure of events and feelings
DOTTED LINE = growth in awareness, self-management skills, and caring
"Negative" and "positive" do not mean good and bad; these terms indicate a
    flow of energy in the polarity of two potent emotions

The Survival Agenda

The survival agenda is most powerful because it is governed by the two most potent human emotions—fear and pleasure seeking. It is not the primary agenda because it is most powerful but because it monopolizes the strongest human emotions. We are born on this agenda and are only able to move off of it as survival needs are met.

Moving from one agenda to another is not complicated once we learn that there is one basic, usually preconscious, question or concern that must be answered adequately before movement to the next higher agenda can occur. Each primary question fits the agenda well. The survival agenda question is: "Am I safe here?" If an individual's perception of safety is not fulfilled, no movement occurs. If, however, adequate security is perceived, movement to the identity agenda is likely.

The key question for the identity agenda is: "Who am I, and what difference do I make?" If an individual's or organization's ego needs are met adequately in a particular situation, or in life in general, movement to the relationship agenda can occur. Notable on this agenda are issues such as competition or jealousy.

The key question for the relationship agenda is: "What's in this (whatever the issue the group is considering) for each of us and all of us together?" We cannot participate in a group appropriately if we are feeling insecure or not being affirmed.

A unique characteristic of human behavior occurs when a person is on an agenda higher than survival. If a threat to survival appears, either instantly or over time, she reverts to the survival agenda and its characteristic emotions and behaviors. However, when the threat passes or is out of sight or no longer perceived, or even when a believable person provides adequate security, she can begin again to move up toward the next highest agenda.

A basic truth about our inner hierarchy of motivational agendas is that we cannot move upward until the key question of each agenda is answered satisfactorily. In order to make such moves we need to answer the key question but must also learn to manage the strong emotions characteristic of each. Fear, for example, is the strongest of all human emotions. When this emotion is stimulated (high alert), it overrides all others. In fact, it is such a strong emotion that it takes a heavy toll on energy and can be sustained for only short periods of time. Stress and anxiety, milder versions of fear, however, consume somewhat less energy and we may endure them for long periods of time with negative consequences delayed, denied, or hidden. The strength of active fear, in any of its forms, is so potent and uncomfortable that we typically try to offset it or escape its consequences by resorting to its opposite emotion on this agenda, namely, pleasure seeking. Eating ("comfort food"), falling asleep, addictions, sex, abusive aggression, demands to be in control of the situation, watching TV or movies, medication are some common stress reducers. Healthier ones are exercise, recreation, meditation, pleasurable tasks, service to others, proper sleep, yoga, energy massage, soothing baths/showers, playing with children, taking adventures with family, and such. But then if we overdo even healthy pleasures, guilt may be triggered (another version of fear), which is likely to generate a repetition of the coping mechanisms just listed.

However, all it often takes to assuage fear is the right stuff, such as reassurances from a significant adult or group, some Scripture passages that bespeak God's care for us, memories of similar situations in which security was achieved, assistance from a good friend or therapist, attendance at an inspiring worship service. This later form of relief is an especially strong reminder for pastors. Pastors need to remember that when preparing the worship service and sermon, it is important to include some forms of reassurances of security, healing, and salvation because it is likely that most of the parishioners attending this service are contending with fear of some kind. And we have just noted that fear is not assuaged unless the "Am I safe here?" question is answered adequately.

You will note in the diagram that an arrow points either upward on one side or downward on the other. Note especially that the arrow pointing downward is more distinct than the one pointing up. This reminds us that the pressure experienced by a person always moves him back down to the survival agenda (dominated by fear and pleasure seeking). This means that unless the answers to the key question of each agenda are consistently positive, a person will eventually revert to the survival agenda.

The Identity Agenda

Most of us are acquainted with the survival agenda even if we are not honest with ourselves about how it affects us. And we have idealized the relationship agenda so much that we forget how difficult it is to reach it and stay on it. But the identity agenda is often the most problematic, for it goes to the meaning of life. The dangers inherent in this agenda include: idolization of ourselves (narcissism), hating ourselves, imagining we are something we are not, not recognizing our special gifts and graces or who we truly are. Then there is the issue of to whom or what do we turn for confirmation of our self-opinion and our needed affirmation.

We should draw a line horizontally through the middle of the diagram (between the anger and the love bracket) to indicate a very important truth about parenting and education in the church. We have assumed for years that love is built into each human being no matter how unloving or unlovable they are. This is not true. The reality is that we are all born with the capacity for love, but whether we shape it negatively or positively is a personal task and a function of learning rather than being simply automatic. All of the emotions below the line through the middle of the diagram are "automatic," that is, we are born with them, while the emotions above the line are all learned emotions. Love is an especially important illustration of this reality.

Some years ago, William Glasser (*Reality Therapy* [New York: Harper & Row, 1965] and his later book *Control Theory* [New York: Harper & Row, 1984]), California therapist, nearly revolutionized the groups of teachers whom he often taught. He showed them by research and models that a child who constantly makes trouble in school or seems to express little kindness or respect is actually acting out his version of love. The reason, according to Glasser, is that when a child does not experience unconditional love, see it exhibited in significant adults, or have his truly loving behavior affirmed, he is likely to learn a negative version of love, which is characteristic of street gangs who as a substitute family love each other, take care of each other, work harmoniously together in gang business such that they may die together. This should be a clear instruction for parents and church school teachers. And, it reminds us that some of the most troublesome persons in a congregation are living out the negative version of love they have learned. Such persons require relationships and training that can guide them into positive expressions of love and reinforce these positive expressions regularly. Nearly every theologian writes of love and every pastor preaches about love, but few seem to understand the emotional dynamics involved in living, teaching, and reinforcing what truly is love.

Note the two emotions that tend to control the identity agenda—anger and love. Anger is problematic for several reasons, for the aggression and abuse it can generate, for the self-doubts and guilt trips, for the stress and extravagant use of energy it entails, and for the barriers it raises to moving up to the relationship agenda. Love, on the other hand, is a favored word in organized religion. We have idealized it to the extent that we often confuse it with being nice, having compassion, engaging in worship, and having sex. More detrimental yet is our assumption that persons should intrinsically know how and actually find ways to love themselves. We know now that healthy self-love (not narcissism) is also learned behavior and thinking, just as is love of family, neighbor, friend, self, and God.

Jesus had a difficult time trying to teach his followers true love, so we should not expect it to be as easy as urging parishioners to love each other more or by saying the word *love* a lot at church. Jesus taught this godlike love by parables (Good Samaritan, Prodigal Son), by slogans ("Love one another . . . as I have loved you"—the Golden Rule), by instruction ("If you love me, keep my commandments," "Love your enemies and do good to them"), by rebuke ("I know that you [Jewish teachers] do not have the love of God in you," "Get behind me, Satan [to Peter], for you are a stumbling block to me"). And finally he taught love by example ("I lay down my life for the sheep," "Love me as I have loved you").

The Relationship Agenda

We've noted some of the characteristics of the survival and identity agendas and their characteristic emotions; now we note the relationship agenda. Here we have sadness and joy as the characteristic agenda markers. Sadness here is neither depression, a bad mood, nor displeasure. It is the true sorrow associated with a relationship that isn't working. This sadness can be a motivator to renew the connection or learn something valuable about human relationships. Or it may, if the host of this emotion feels abandoned (down to identity agenda) or threatened (down to survival agenda), lead to totally losing faith in relationships. The relationship agenda is a sensitive and nurturing agenda. Thriving relationships are marked by respectful interactions, synergy to achieve goals not possible for one person alone, and compassionate caring for each other. Thriving relationships give birth to more thriving relationships that grow in depth and scope and produce joy that not only nurtures but also generates lives full of meaning and service.

With the key issues represented by the other two agendas (security and self-confidence) satisfied, the relationship agenda offers many of the positive characteristics of a normal or paradigmatic congregation. For with those threatening issues managed healthfully, our personal and corporate energies and resources are available to handle even complicated relationships and shared responsibilities. This agenda, as noted, is marked by several spiritual graces such as respect for others. Respect is a grace that allows us to accept others as they are (diversity, impairment, disagreement, superior brainpower, wealth, inexperience in the Christian life and teachings, and such).

Openness is another of the positive graces of this agenda. It does not mean willingness to accept all ideas, conditions, or tasks. Rather, it means a willingness to listen and explore other ideas than our own. Creativity flourishes in the presence of this grace. When these graces and attitudes are operant, the soul of the organization, as well as individual souls, remains healthy.

Openness is a popular concept. Without question it is a positive dynamic of body-mind-spirit health. Yet, again we must manage it with caution, well-known now to persons who have become victims of being open to the point of unhealthiness. What "seems like a good idea at the time" can become detrimental or mislead us. An example I use in my seminars on the subject of openness and consequences came from a youth evangelist. He tells of preaching to an auditorium full of self-affirmed Christian young people. During the course of his message, he spoke of the folly of lying and asked everyone who believed lying was wrong to raise their hands. Nearly everyone raised their hands. Then he asked all those who had lied to avoid bad consequences to raise their hands. Nearly the same number raised their hands. He then asked if any in the audience saw a disconnect between the first response and the second. With a unified voice the audience said, "No!" The rest of his message was devoted to asking them to reconsider the disconnect between their beliefs and their behavior. There is currently a global movement in ethics that is based solely on consequences; sometimes it is called consequential ethics and its power cannot be overemphasized. And yet, we cannot ignore the power for good as people take the consequences of their behavior more seriously and hold each other accountable for them.

Generosity is yet another of the positive graces of this agenda. Goodwill and compassion flourish in the presence of this grace. Stewardship is traditionally linked to generosity. However, stewardship has become so deeply associated solely with church pledges and habitual gifts that it often misses the joy of generosity—generosity of time, of attention, of money, of resources, of service. The relationship agenda is enormously valuable in the life of normal and paradigmatic congregations, and can be part of the healing and continued health of those that are dysfunctional or even toxic.

Perspective

These "Agendas of Human Behavior" are one of the most useful reminders of how complicated human life and relationships are and yet how they can be managed positively by learning how they work. They are present all the time, in each human being and in each congregation, whether we recognize them or not. Leaders of congregations must take seriously the task of recognizing which agenda is dominant for a congregation at a particular time. And they must learn to help a congregation move from an inappropriate agenda to one that serves present needs and God's purposes best. For when we ignore the agenda, we are likely to encounter resistance and conflict when we want consensual decisions and ministries.

The Ethics of Consequences

As far as we know, there have always been moral rules for human behavior, some made by the environment (Don't hunt lions without a big spear), some made by authority figures ("God says thou shalt not . . ."), and some made by group consensus (Let's don't steal each other's cattle). We still have such rules; when these rules or principles are codified we call it ethics. But the real determiners for behaviors, often despite the principles, are *consequences*. For example, Christian principles declare that attendance at worship on Sunday is mandatory. But when the day is glorious and golf buddies must play during the worship time, the choice between the principle of faithful attendance at worship and its satisfactions must compete with the experience of a golf outing with its pleasures. Both choices have consequences, yet one will predominate. So principles and pleasures are both based on consequences. This is why the highly principled life must be based on spiritual/moral principles that are deeply engrained and trusted. Otherwise the choice that offers the highest immediate pleasure is likely to be chosen.

Why include the field of ethics in a discussion of unhealthy and healthy congregations? Good question and keep asking it, for an awareness of the historical, philosophical panorama of formal and informal ethics is a significant aid in seeing the ways human understandings of how to relate to each other appropriately have changed. For centuries great minds considered the best way to manage our relationships and then offered guidelines and rationalizations that guided generations of people.

Are there relational rules for congregations? Yes. Where do they come from? More and more they are coming from the global society. And no matter the claims of church officials, politicians, academics, lawyers, and parents—the rules come from a kind of consensus in our human environment. We are slowly realizing that laws made by officialdom no longer keep up with the changes, needs, and motivations of society. Though we all try to obey good rules and avoid hurting each other, the one true reality in ethics is the consequences of human behavior. Laws make pronouncements; principles offer standards, but consequences happen. This is true in government, schools, businesses, families, and congregations. We try to choose our consequences and may choose to worry about the rules later.

Readers who study the formal discipline of ethics will recognize that we are delving into an ancient and current field of scholarship. I leave the complete review of this elegant field to readers who love it as I do. I introduce ethics here briefly because it makes a most important point about understanding why people, especially church people, act like they do.

Secularly oriented persons have only the general laws and regulations of society, plus whatever professional standards they must follow, in making their behavioral and lifelong decisions. Christians, on the other hand, make decisions according to the Bible, much of it based on Jewish law, the moral teachings of Jesus, plus the ethical accretions of organized religion, these are added to society's laws and any professional standards. Both secular and Christian persons often assume that the ethics they believe and try to live by are universally applicable. Many thoughtful persons now, however, are realizing that the wisdom of our beliefs are limited, and they are more willing to let those who believe differently have more freedom to do so.

The ethical decision-making process for believers can become complicated and even dangerous as they sort through this mix for a significant decision. And this is one of the reasons more and more decisions by Christians resemble those of secular persons. This can make for serious conflict in a congregation between those who see a distinctive "Christian" decision versus one that is similar to the decision a secular person makes. Abortion, birth control, and gay-lesbian-bisexual-transgender issues are examples where each person may make a moral decision that may conflict with that of another parishioner or the pastor. The idea that Christians may come down on different sides of an issue is not fully appreciated by many congregations. More than one pastor has been abused or fired over such conflicts.

In the history of ethics there are essentially two mainstreams of thought. One is a constantly changing set of theories such as idealism, stoicism, hedonism, realism, deontological systems, logical positivism to name a representative few. The other stream focuses on consequences such as empiricism, utilitarianism, pragmatism, and such. It is interesting to note that belief systems with all their interesting innovations were matched sooner or later by another version of practical ethics that emphasized consequences as the significant reference for ethical decision making.

And so today, ethics and morality are again dominated by consequences as the ultimate reference point. Though there are sharp divisions between the absolutist ("my ethics are universal") and consequential ("we all have to live with each other's consequences") believers, it is difficult to sustain either view as ultimate for every situation. For beliefs can be wrong or ambiguous, and consequences can be unintended, unknown, or connected to other consequences. (See appendix C.)

Ethics plays a significant part in the prescriptive chapter to follow. It will be obvious that prescriptions for healing or health in congregations require wise combinations of sincere beliefs and a recognition of the consequences of human behavior. Based on even the simple evidence of this book, we are reminded that detoxification, restoration of functionality, patching up normalcy, and nurturing a paradigmatic congregation must run the gauntlet of human motivations. Motivations are the power dynamics of a person's behavior. They often overpower the best of intentions, good-faith agreements, and even common sense. Therefore, before we begin the prescriptive chapter, we must recognize that any good change we need or want in a congregation must have a foundation of at least minimally trained leaders, a courageous and healthy pastor, and parishioners who are willing to seek healing or strive to become a better congregation than they already are.

Relevant Behavior Factors

Inherent motivations and the current ethics of consequences are not the only determiners of human behavior, of course. Following is a limited list of other influences on human behavior that should be factored into our understanding of motivations. They help enhance the understanding of the prescriptions to come.

Engrams are one such influence. An engram is a theoretical construct explaining how we build and retain distinct memories and definitions of experiences, objects, and pertinent details of something important to us. (For a more scientific explanation, see Daniel J. Siegel, *The Developing Mind* [New York: The Guilford Press, 1999], pp. 27, 28, or John J. Ratey, *A User's Guide to the Brain* [New York: Vintage Books, 2001], pp. 311ff.)

The term *engram* is not a familiar one to many, though it is a perfectly valid theoretical term in brain-mind research. Why include this term in a discussion of the sicknesses and health of congregations? Good question . . . keep on asking it, for it is a valuable concept in helping us understand where people get their ideas about important issues and why they resist ideas and strategies for the congregation that they don't like. The phrase "long-term memory" could be used, but it is cumbersome, too general, and also difficult to explain. Engram is a short word with its meaning built into the word: "en" means in or into, "gram" means a record.

Engrams usually originate in a strong experience that our brain retains in its long-term memories because this event, object, or relationship seems important to us. If an engram remains significant for us, we add other relevant memories and information to it until it becomes a reference point for thinking about anything closely related to it. For example, our engram of God probably began with a strong impression of the meaning the word *God*, to which we have added further impressions, experiences, and teachings. After this engram is established, depending on when and how we experienced God or teachings about God, we say the word without much thought, but can offer definitions and ideas if asked. And, in a conflict with someone who believes differently about God, we would be ready to defend the engram, assuming we are defending God. The same process and conflict pertains to any other engram we feel strongly about, for example, defending the pastor, or contending for the use of inclusive language, or resisting the new hymnal, or opposing the Instrument of Peace because it threatens *our* control of the church board.

Each engram is a function of the experiences and long-term accretions for the individual in whose mind it exists. This engram may be similar to or quite different from the engram of the same entity in another person's mind. Further, since it is retained in our long-term memory, it is difficult to change it without strong new impressions. (It should be noted that the idea of an engram is accepted by many authorities, for example, Howard Gardner, *The Mind's New Science* [New York: BasicBooks, 1985], pp. 262 ff.) Nevertheless, we know from experience that our minds have iconic definitions and memories stored as references for any significant person, experience, or entity. So we shall retain this term to aid in the understanding of individual engrams of a particular congregation.

Our engrams, as well as our beliefs and our awareness of consequences, are not free of bias, prejudice, misinterpretation, or the insights of experience. Just as all of the stimuli that are received through our senses are immediately interpreted, to some degree, in our brain-mind before they become fully conscious, so our beliefs and sense of consequences are modified immediately by the long-term memories of significant experiences and teachings stored in our minds. Some theorists call these long-term memories *engrams*. These become our reference points for decision making, and include both our beliefs and consequences. For example, as stated above, our belief about God is an engram. Each of us has composed and stored a mental picture and beliefs about Deity that becomes our God. Since none of us has seen God, we must settle for beliefs about "Mysterium Tremendum," *autopoesis* (Rudolf Otto), the I AM encountered by Moses as recorded in the Bible, and the teachings of Jesus regarding the Creator-Parent God. In the global interactions of religions, the competition to define and impose a singular engram of God resembles the tragic "theological cleansings" in many congregations and some denominations.

Each member of a congregation, including the pastor, denominational officials, and the neighborhood, has a personal, unique, and iconic engram of their congregation in mind every time she or he thinks of it, or considers issues that affect it. This is another version of the "virtual" (Internet) congregation discussed in an earlier chapter. Both have been developed in a person's mind. Yet, the virtual congregation is a function of the Internet and its experiences, while an engram is a mental picture of this congregation in its material setting, history, and ministries. Note again the emphasis in this book on what goes on in people's minds regarding their congregation, and how this literally governs how they participate. For those who want to aid an ailing congregation or nurture a thriving one, having a relevant understanding of how parishioners think is invaluable.

As has already been noted, what goes on in our minds is directly relevant to our souls. If our soul is healthy, our thoughts will usually be healthy. Similarly, what goes on in a congregation is directly relevant to its soul. If the congregational soul is healthy, it will usually generate healing, appropriate spiritual nurture, and perpetuate godly ministries.

Culture

Culture is a familiar term indicating a particular group behaving and believing in unique ways and occupying a specific geographical location over time. This is a generic term with a generally understood meaning. In recent years, however, it has taken on more specific meanings. There is the IBM culture, the Washington, D.C. culture, the Taliban culture, the Boy Scout culture, the dot-com culture, the gay-lesbian-bisexual-transgender culture, and the NRA culture, among thousands of others. In prior generations these were called subcultures and viewed as simply specialized groups within a larger culture, usually ethnic, continental, or national. Organized religion (the major religions) was for centuries viewed as both a subculture within a national or geographical culture and yet as a kind of global culture. Recently religion has begun to follow secular models of cultures, such as those just listed. Each congregation, even in highly structured denominations, is tending to become its own subculture, or culture in the new limited meaning of this term. This is significant for our concern for working with individual congregations that are toxic, dysfunctional, normal, or paradigmatic, because each congregation, no matter its larger connections, now is a culture.

This new understanding of the term *culture* has come out of business management, sociology, economics, anthropology, and Internet associations. Due to the declining control of congregations by denominational structures, the ebb and flow of membership, and the waning of financial resources, congregations have become more autonomous.

Interestingly, new secular definitions of culture have a markedly religious flavor. For example, Edgar H. Schein (in *Organizational Culture and Leadership*, 2nd ed. [San Francisco: Jossey-Bass, 1992], p. 12) defines the culture as "A pattern of shared basic assumptions that the group learned as it solved its problems of external adaptation and internal integration, that has worked well enough to be considered valid, and, therefore, to be taught to new members as the correct way to perceive, think, and feel in relation to those problems." Sounds like a description of many of our congregations that have resorted to the "problem-solving" technique of managing themselves, doesn't it?

Another example: Peg Neuhauser, et al. (in their *Culture.com* [Toronto: John Wiley & Sons, 2000], pp. 4, 5) say a corporate culture is sharing underlying assumptions as core values, with acceptable behaviors and habits at a secondary level, and with symbols and language at the most visible level (my paraphrase). This sounds more like one of our normal congregations.

Yet another example, this one from quantum sciences: Margaret Wheatley, *Leadership and the New Science* (San Francisco: Berrett-Koehler Publishers, 1999), 20, 84ff.: A culture is a self-organizing, living system marked by *autopoesis* (see glosssary). in that it remains consistent within itself as it adapts to environment, and generates what it needs for renewal and continuing existence. Again, this is my paraphrase of a long, complicated description of any contemporary organization. When an organization knows who it is, what its strengths are, and what it is trying to accomplish, it can respond intelligently to changes in its environment. Whatever it decides to do is determined by this clear sense of self, not just by a new trend. This internal strength and openness to its environment give it capacities to shape its environment. This is called *autopoesis*.

This broad definition provides another and very compatible understanding of the soul of an organization (cf. the definitions of soul in the introduction). Note that the internal functioning of the organization generates a consistent flow of energy devoted to the health and purposes of the organization. Note that it is open to change, but only so far as it incorporates changes that are consistent with its purposes. Note further that this strength of healthy identity and outflow of energy bring healthy changes to its environment.

Autopoesis becomes another name for the soul of a healthy, paradigmatic congregation. Its soul is made and kept healthy, in part, by the individual souls that compose its spiritual corpus. But remember the soul of a congregation is always greater than the sum of the souls of its individual members. And this corporate health tends to keep the individual souls healthy. It is apparent that this two-way process mirrors the healthy spiritual chaos of interaction, adaptation, and generativeness. Health is used to produce health. Energy is used to generate energy. And identity is used as discipleship for service and salvation.

Close observation of such a congregation discloses an internal process called *mimesis* (literally "imitation" in Greek). It is a dynamic that occurs naturally in a healthy environment, such as God's unexploited creation. Ancient philosophers and scientists observed it as the healthy way nature preserves and adapts itself. More recently, philosophers such as René Girard (*Violence and the Sacred*) and his American protégé Gil Bailie (*Violence Unveiled*) have provided an analysis of human history, demonstrating how humanity has learned and relearned violence from the worst of models instead of the best, Jesus the Christ. We see how easily unhealthy people become prone to violence in every form because of the models to which they are exposed so regularly. Christianity and its Christ is the perfected alternative that brings us back to imitating the best in God's creation for the health of all.

In *Learned Optimism*, Martin Seligman (New York: Simon and Schuster, 1990) shows us step by step how we may learn the positive side of living, in contrast to his earlier book. His earlier book showed how we learn to imitate the unhealthy behavior fostered by abuse and violence until we become helpless to do anything but repeat hopeless aggressions. It is clear from human history and the warnings of the mimesis writings that when we imitate the wrong models we become sick and toxic to others. Yet, when the great models of Christianity and healthy congregations are present, we see that body-mind-spirit health can be learned by imitation (discipleship) as readily as unhealthiness to the benefit of all.

Summary

In this chapter we turned from illustrative congregations to insights from human motivations. The most primitive and yet hopeful sweep of insights comes from the agendas of human behavior, which show how human beings become sickened when their negative emotions control their thinking and lifestyle and how they become the best that they can be when their lives are dominated by positive emotions.

Next we reviewed the contemporary amalgamation of ethics and morality into a general attitude of "pick your consequences," as shown by the earlier analysis of consequential ethics outlined in appendix C.

Attention shifted then to the brain-mind icons often called engrams. These are the solidified, cumulative memories and learnings that become our reference points for decision making and development of our lifestyles in personal lives and in congregations.

Culture, in its contemporary meanings, was our next insight into human motivations. Here we noted groups of persons gathered for a significant purpose constitute themselves into an organization that develops a life of its own, which can either be sick or healthy, depending on the internal behavior of its constituents and its environment.

Finally, we noted the power of models and imitation, recognizing again that with realistic, positive models and reinforcement through spiritual nurture, we can develop healthy individual and corporate souls.

CHAPTER SIX

Instruments of Peace

Prescriptions and remedies have a welcome place in congregations as well as in hospitals and doctors' offices. For generations congregations were expected to function appropriately on their own, according to the traditions of their parent denomination. Since the new era of entitlement thinking and consequential ethics, however, the internal discipline of congregations has often been inadequate to manage the conflicts arising from independent thinking, loss of respect for the authority of the clergy role, increase of diversity, and loss of confidence and satisfaction with traditional congregational worship and programs. Seminaries and denominational training have been inadequate to meet the new leadership requirements. All of these changes contribute to the increase in dysfunction and conflict.

The good news, however, is that many religious leaders sense and follow the Holy Spirit into new forms of spirituality, and they are open to innovation. Further, we have a highly competent class of leaders and consultants available to provide information and guidance for handling both the new problems and the new opportunities.

Of concern, however, is the lack of basic guidelines for keeping a congregation healthy in the midst of infectious evil and attractive fads. Experienced leaders are rediscovering the value of laying a foundation of guidelines for keeping peace in congregations, for training lay leaders in discipleship and management, and for supporting pastors in their efforts to preach and model the presence of God in the midst of the community of faith (soul).

This chapter provides needed protocols and reminders of healthy congregational interactions. Thus far this book has presented cases that illustrate toxicity and breakdowns in congregational functioning, reported ordinary and exemplary congregational functioning, both positive and negative, and highlighted the human motivations behind change, breakdowns, and health. Now, new prescriptions and familiar guidelines for spiritual nurture are offered in brief form to encourage pastors and congregations to develop practical, local ways that bring healing and opportunities to help congregations thrive through joyful ministries. In this book these are called Instruments of Peace. The first and presently most important of these is called Grievance-Suggestion Procedure (GSP).

In keeping with the medical and biological metaphors of this book, the GSP is essentially an immunization. It is most effective when studied, installed, and used *before* there is serious conflict. And like many inoculations against a serious disorder, occasionally congregations need booster shots. So given our short memories and the many issues coming before boards and congregations, the GSP must be reviewed and studied with a practice case (see the "Conflict Over Healing" case in the appendixes) periodically, so it is ready for effective use when needed.

Instruments of Peace

The Hebrew term *shalom* has become a focusing word in contemporary spirituality. It has at least three translated meanings: "peace," "wholeness," "salvation." All of these concepts offer valuable insights into the mystery of spirituality. Yet each needs a directive for action, lest it remain only an idea that seemed good at the time. A directive for action, a recipe, an instrument that can facilitate shalom is needed for our real-life congregational situations.

The values and dangers of reducing any aspect of spirituality to a formula, ritual, symbol, or instrumentality are mostly apparent. Having an instrument of peace is similar to having an instrument of war. Waging war is not a fantasy; it takes place in specific locations, using instruments of warfare. Peace also is not just fantasy. It takes place when people wage peace—with instruments, strategies, and a sense of mission.

The well-known "Prayer of St. Francis of Assisi" begins, "Lord, make me an instrument of your peace." Spiritually disciplined persons are agents (instruments) of peace. That is certainly part of the peace process. But this instruction is about strategy and procedure rather than persons acting as agents of peace. Such persons are vital to the health of any congregation. And they need tools—instruments—for facilitating peace. The whole congregation needs to know about such instruments so all may participate in the peace and health of the congregation.

This is all relevant to the dynamics of conflict and abuse occurring in organized religion today. We are learning that we must rethink—reinvent—our definitions, strategies, instruments, and mission if we are to be cocreators with God of a kingdom of peace-health-salvation. And we are learning that we must have new instruments of peace that fit contemporary spiritual warfare.

Context

Peace, health, and salvation should be normal, even automatic, in the church, according to our idealized thinking. This fantasy, however, can be a barrier to realistic thinking about the community of faith. But the escalation of conflict and abuse in congregations and denominations is a reality check. It reminds us that spiritual warfare is a reality. Those who are unprepared will become casualties.

Besides the dawning awareness of spiritual warfare, we are also required by contemporary realities to rethink our common understandings of the basic concepts of shalom mentioned earlier. *Peace*, for example, is not just the absence of conflict and warfare. Many have learned that peace must be waged by dedicated actions. And peace is not a time to settle into self-serving indulgence; it is a time to heal, nurture and grow. *Health* is not just absence of pain and disease; it is wholeness in the biblical sense, which means fitness for God's purposes. *Salvation* is not just a guarantee of eternal bliss. It is God's redemption of humankind coupled with our dedicated service in caring for others, and redeeming our resources in the model of Jesus Christ.

In addition to these fresh insights regarding the basics of spirituality, we are learning that peacemaking and peacekeeping are sustained by both spiritual disciplines and discerning strategies. We are learning to care about prevention and be proactive with battle strategies and triage. This context helps us understand the what, why, how, when, and who of sustaining shalom. The rest of this instruction is devoted to discussing a particular instrument of peace that appears to be valuable in our stewardship of shalom in congregations.

The Grievance-Suggestion Procedure

In consultations with troubled congregations and the pastoral care of pastors, I find that a valuable tool or instrument is typically missing that could prevent much conflict and could provide a method of resolving much of the conflict and abuse that is occurring. That tool is a clear, concise, and workable method of handling grievances and suggestions for change within the congregation. Without such an instrument congregational leaders and pastors are left with the possibilities of anarchy, manipulation by congregational powerbrokers, or patching together whatever seems like a good idea at the time. We can do better than this.

We can call such an instrument a grievance-suggestion procedure (GSP, for brevity). This means a well-known and readily available channel for guiding both concerns and suggestions for change through an accountable and caring process of consideration and resolution. It is valuable to use the same method for handling both complaints and suggestions for change in the congregation. For this allows the procedure to be used and perceived as a positive way of handling both the negative and positive concerns of the parishioners.

When I deal with this issue in the seminars on managing the clergy-killer phenomenon, a participant often expresses discomfort with the terminology of "grievance." This is a valid concern that can be addressed by changing the name of the procedure for that congregation. There is no magic in the terminology. I use the term *grievance* because it expresses the urgent unhappiness of some parishioners who are angry about something in the congregation. If the complaint is actually a negatively worded request for a particular change, the GSP will handle it as a suggestion for change rather than a grievance.

Since it is not common for a congregation (or a denomination) to have a simple, clear, practical procedure for handling grievances and suggestions for change, it will likely be useful to consider the generic questions that arise when an unfamiliar strategy is suggested.

It is best not to be too literal here in suggesting the contents of a GSP, for each congregation has unique needs, polity, bylaws, and traditions. We can, however, list typical ingredients that are useful.

1. The GSP should be designated as the official process for handling all grievances and suggestions for change. This means it must be officially voted by duly elected representatives of the congregation. The only exceptions are those allowed by a similar official action.
2. The grievance or suggestion must be submitted in writing.
3. It must be signed.
4. It must be dated.
5. The GSP should name a specific person or officer to whom it must be submitted.
6. The GSP should indicate what official entity (committee, council, etc.) of the congregation or denomination will review and decide on the grievance-suggestion.
7. The GSP should indicate what official responses can be expected and when the submitter will be notified of official actions and decisions.
8. The GSP should indicate that decisions of the official board conclude the matter, unless an officially designated appeal process is followed.
9. The GSP should state that anyone not abiding by such judgment will be held accountable for such behavior, and how they will be held accountable.

It should be obvious that each congregation should have a GSP that fits its own circumstances and yet, promotes peace, decorum, and faithful ministries. It is not the goal of a GSP to produce perfect harmony. This, of course, is not a realistic expectation among normal persons. Diversity, disagreements, dislikes, and mistakes—even sin—are expected and anticipated human dynamics. Conflict is not all bad, but abuse is unacceptable. Conflict is often positive and valuable, clarifying disagreements and encouraging creativity where grace is operant.

Some of what constitutes a GSP is common sense, civility, and caring. There are precedents and guidelines for the content of a GSP in the denomination's polity, the congregation's bylaws, and in such general resources as *Robert's Rules of Order*. All of these have standing in church tribunals and secular courts of law, as do many other documents that are signed and dated. It is important that the GSP conform to the denomination's polity. Actions that violate official polity may be nullified. And actions that violate a congregation's bylaws are illegal and may be overturned in secular courts.

Since the church is a mission under God rather than a business or a social organization, it is important that its governance be based on Scripture and spiritual disciplines. Therefore, the GSP should begin with references to the need for congregational decisions to be enveloped in sincere and humble prayer, and suggestions for appropriate passages from the Bible to be quoted and studied. It can be very helpful to begin the GSP with quotations from, or references to, Matthew 18, Acts 15, 1 Corinthians 12 and 13, Galatians 5:13–6:5, Philippians 2:1-7, Colossians 3:1-10, and 1 Thessalonians 4:12-22.

If harm (sin) has been done, then the forgiveness formula must be invoked. This five-step formula, derived from Scripture, will be presented later. We should remember, of course, that the hard-core terrorists of the church—the clergy killers—are unlikely to participate in any forgiveness and healing process. This does not fit their purposes. Often then, the congregation and pastor must do the forgiveness process and the healing without the perpetrator's participation. But such painful and, yet, healing processes underscore the need for a GSP. Much hurt, sin, and lost opportunities can be avoided if the congregation has and uses a GSP.

In seminars I am asked often for a specific example of a GSP. Such a request indicates how poorly prepared most of us are to lead our congregations in clear, precise, and practical strategies for handling the sensitive issue of conflict and change. There is no one formula that will be perfect for every congregation. But each congregation has a denominational polity, bylaws, and tradition. It should, of course, also have common sense and spiritual disciplines that can guide us toward God's purposes instead of self-serving struggles to get our way at the expense of others. Yet in these days of change, conflict, and abuse, it is obvious that each congregation needs some form of an effective GSP. Many congregations are floundering at the mercy of nefarious powerbrokers who have little intention of seeking God's purposes rather than their own. Therefore, it appears that a primary responsibility of spiritual leaders these days is to aid a congregation in preparing a GSP, one that will guide leaders and congregations when there is conflict, and which is also prophylactic.

Since it may be helpful for spiritual leaders to see an actual GSP in print, I have compiled some basic ingredients into a generic model of a GSP, as follows.

A Model Grievance-Suggestion Procedure

Good communications are a characteristic of a spiritually healthy congregation. And one of the most important communications between people has to do with managing disagreements and making suggestions for change. We want to be a spiritually healthy congregation. Therefore, the elected leadership of the church provides the following procedure for handling such sensitive issues.

We begin with guidance from the Scriptures. In Matthew 18:15-20 we have a three-step procedure taught by Jesus to his disciples. Where there is a grievance between two persons, Jesus taught, the harmed person should go to the person who harmed him and seek redress in private. This first step is optional, depending on the likelihood of abuse from the offender. If no solution occurs, bring witnesses and try again. If the person behaving in unhealthy ways will not repent, bring it before the congregation. And if the offender still does not repent, the whole community of faith is to treat that person as unrepentant.

These are hard teachings, but they are from no less than Jesus the Christ. The process and rationale are clear. Persons who insist on disrupting the harmony of the congregation and are unrepentant must not be allowed to infect others with their spiritual sickness.

The early church also gave us a valuable model for handling suggestions for change in the community of faith. In Acts 15:1-34 we have a record of the first general convention of the church after the death and resurrection of Jesus. Some members wanted to make changes in theology and practice, which others opposed. The Apostles Paul and Peter convened a meeting of the church leaders where with prayer and respect for each other they discussed the options. Then they negotiated changes in theology and practice to which all could agree (*consensus*). And because of this prayerful process, the early church thereafter grew rapidly and healthfully.

Those methods from centuries ago may not work exactly for our congregation today. But they provide a context of caring and respect, of prayerful dialogue, negotiation, tough-minded spirituality, and of sincere seeking of God's will rather than our own. In order to apply these spiritual principles to our congregation, we provide the following stated steps for handling grievances and suggestions for change.

1. This procedure has been developed prayerfully, after careful review of our denomination's polity, our congregation's bylaws,

and our traditions and present circumstances. Since it has been voted on and passed by duly assembled members of this congregation and its spiritual leaders, it is the only procedure that is acceptable for handling grievances and suggestions for change.

2. Any grievance or suggestion for change must be submitted in writing. If assistance is needed to meet this requirement, it will be provided by elders or deacons of this congregation.

3. The person initiating the action and any associates who wish to participate in this action must sign the written document.

4. This document must indicate the date on which it is properly submitted.

5. A *grievance* must be submitted in this documented form to the chairperson of the personnel committee if it is focused on a member of the church staff, or to the chairperson of the board if there is no personnel committee. If it is focused on a parishioner or a member of the board, it should be directed to the chairperson of the board. And if a *suggestion for change* is submitted, it should be directed to the chairperson of the board.

6. The board shall review and deliberate the documented issue according to its commonly accepted practice, and render a decision, unless it chooses to delegate this responsibility to another official group in the congregation, or select an *ad hoc* group for this purpose. All such deliberations and decisions shall be reported to the board in writing, and may be reviewed and acted upon by the board. In any case, the board retains final authority for a decision on this documented issue.

7. The person(s) submitting a documented grievance or suggestion for change may be asked to appear before the board or its designee for purposes of clarification. In any case, this person(s) will be notified in writing of the board's decisions regarding this documented issue within 90 days from the date of submission, which appears on the document.

8. The decisions of the board are final, unless appealed by the following process:
   a. The issue may be resubmitted one time only, according to the above procedure, and will be accepted for reconsideration only if presented with significant new data and information.

b. After this issue has been appealed to the board one time, the board's decision(s) may be appealed to the denomination's nearest office, according to denominational polity.

9. A decision by the board, whether in its original deliberations or after one official appeal, is final. If an appeal is made to the denominational office, its decision is final. There shall be no further presentation of this issue verbally, or by document, or by abusive conversation, at any time. Violation of this procedure shall be considered grounds for initiation of a trial within the tribunals of the denomination's or the congregation's polity for all persons violating the board's or the denomination's decision(s) regarding this issue. If this issue is submitted to secular courts of law, all parties shall follow the mandates of such courts, unless the board or denomination duly determine to initiate contrary actions, and are willing to sustain lawful consequences.

10. All persons involved in the above process are responsible for their own prayerful Christian conduct and attitude during the handling of any GSP. It is expected that all parishioners and their spiritual leaders shall regard each other with love and respect, even during times of stressful conflict. It is also expected that official decisions of the board and denomination will be honored fully, whether agreed with or not, for we all function under God's authority, and believe that the board's and denomination's decisions are made under this authority. Anyone unable to maintain such attitudes and behavior is expected to prayerfully reconsider their commitment to this congregation, or to transfer their membership to another congregation.

Implementation of the GSP

The Grievance-Suggestion Procedure (GSP) is a clear, simple, workable process for handling positive suggestions for change in a congregation's ministries, programs, and governance, as well as concerns, grievances, and dissent. The GSP is a stepwise method that promotes orderly, reliable resolution of potentially divisive matters before they become contentious or abusive. Though this is a tested and reliable protocol, its effectiveness depends on trained leadership, consistent implementation, and positive congregational communications.

This GSP is only a model. It must be interpreted and adapted for particular settings. When the training, implementation, and advocacy are done well, the adapted GSP generates a healthy congregational attitude toward diversity, change, and mission. The GSP should be presented in a context of biblical insights and appropriate influences from the parent denomination's polity and the congregation's bylaws.

Following are the suggested steps for implementing the GSP:

1. Study the model: read, discuss, probe, explore expectations and options.
2. Seek consensual approval of the idea, the format, and possible uses.
3. Assign writing of a draft adapting the model to this congregation.
4. Review the draft with elected officials, and use consultants if necessary.
5. Complete revisions, training, and final official approval from governing body.
6. Generate a plan for implementation.
7. Review the plan for implementation, and secure governing body approval.
8. Advocate and explain the final version to the congregation. Allow for feedback and discussion, then set a date for the model to become official policy.
9. Notify the denominational office of this action.
10. Continue advocacy, reminders, and celebrations of congregational health and peace.

Congratulations! These steps provide a simple, clear and workable method for managing diversity, disagreements, and suggestions for change, with respect for one another, a peaceable consensus, and spiritual energy saved for mission.

The Forgiveness Formula

Another Instrument of Peace is the ancient and respected Forgiveness Formula. Forgiveness is a spiritual-mental grace taught and modeled by Jesus, and for centuries has been part of organized religion's sacraments, worship, and ministries practices. Yet it is used in practical ways so seldom these days. Few sacrificial decisions, by individuals and congregations, are as powerful in providing healing and spiritual growth as the decision to forgive. And this grace is so available to those who live as disciples of Jesus Christ. Forgiveness can be given any time of day or night, with any person or persons, alone or with the community of faith, and repeated.

Forgiveness is so powerful in everyday life and interpersonal relationships that it has become a featured subject for discussion in the mental health professions. There is a good reason mental health professionals are using forgiveness in therapy so frequently now—it is great therapy! It is discouraging to see that mainline Christianity doesn't seem to know how to use forgiveness to generate peace—among marriage partners, among competitive youth, among longtime enemies, and among parishioners who disagree or have hurt one another.

We know, some from experience, that forgiving a serious wrong is very difficult, especially if it caused serious harm and collateral damage. Yet Jesus makes it plain that forgiveness is not an option, it is a requirement of discipleship (Matt 5:44, Luke 6:37). Jesus modeled it in his most painful hour (Luke 23:34), and it is part of the Lord's Prayer we say so easily.

The Forgiveness Formula can and should be preached, taught, and practiced regularly. Its simplicity makes that easy. But its practice can be so painful that sometimes it must be practiced with the aid of clergy, prayerful friends, or a Christian therapist. The rewards in healing and peace of mind are dramatic. When practiced, it nurtures the individual soul, as well as the soul of the congregation. When not practiced, it leaves opening for hatred, fear, vengeance, and other harmful stresses. The pain of a serious grievance never goes away, unless forgiveness brings release.

The Steps of the Forgiveness Formula

1. *Hear the Gospel.* In this first step we take time to read, hear, and review what the gospel says about the importance of forgiveness. This is such a powerful first step that it should be a regular part of congregational life, not only the confession-absolution of the liturgy, but the actual practice of forgiveness in marriage, family, school, even nations (e.g., Archbishop Desmond Tutu).
2. *Accepting Forgiveness.* This second step opens the door to the rest. We must accept the forgiveness God offers us, and learn to translate that into forgiving ourselves.

3. *Confession-Forgiveness of the Sin.* This can either be my confession to someone or theirs to me. It works best when both confess, assuming both have done damage. But if I have been wronged, I can help make it possible for the perpetrator to confess to me and ask forgiveness. The most difficult part of the forgiveness occurs when the perpetrator (real or perceived) refuses to confess and ask forgiveness or even acknowledge to wrongdoing. This means the rest of the formula must be completed alone, with God's grace. For when we must forgive without a confession from the perpetrator, we must reach into God's forgiveness, which has already occurred for me and so many others, and turn this grievance into a gift of God's grace, until I am able to forgive also and let go of the pain and stress.

4. *Doing Penance (restitution).* We seldom seem to even get to the confession forgiveness part, much less to the restitution. And if we do, restitution can become quite complicated. Therefore when the penance stage is reached, all participants need a special blessing of God's grace to handle it well.

5. *Pronouncing Absolution.* We know God forgives and "remembers our sins no more." Can we do the same? Probably not the total forgetting part, but we can one day say, "I forgive you through God's grace of forgiveness offered to all. In so doing I relinquish my grievance and the stress it generates."

6. *Achieving Reconciliation.* This step in the forgiveness formula is problematical. So much depends upon the individual ability of each participant. When there is a consensual understanding of these progressive steps, and each participant is recovered well enough to make a realistic commitment to the new relationship, reconciliation allows growing freedom from the consequences of the grievance. This process must be mutual, not be coerced, and amenable to review. Justice is a key issue here, especially in the case of physical or sexual abuse. Therapists and persons serving in an alter ego role must be involved when abuse has occurred. And the victim/survivor must have full power over any decision for face-to-face meetings or other arrangements for resolution of the full forgiveness formula.

The Forgiveness Formula is a potent Instrument of Peace. It should have its place in our repertory of grace-filled living more often.

Healing Ministries

Organized religion must take its place alongside medicine, mental therapy, and even alternative or complementary medicine, in leading the health crusade that is gaining strength across the United States. For only the church can speak with holy authority of the healing power of prayer, the sacraments, and the support of the community of faith. Without spiritual healing, no healing is complete. Research is beginning to demonstrate this, but we as disciples of Jesus the Healer must proclaim and practice it.

In my seminary training, I don't recall hearing much mention of healing and never saw a healing service. Healing is still a nonissue in many seminaries, for organized religion turned physical health over to science about the time of the Renaissance and has made little effort to participate since, except for some charismatic or evangelical practitioners. Curiously, nearly every leading medical school now has at least one class on spirituality and healing.

When I do seminars I usually ask that some time be set apart for at least a brief healing service. I have never been refused. Most often, the healing service becomes a high point in the seminar.

Since we have so little training and participation in healing, we should note some guidelines for those who have little experience:

1. Places of worship are not hospitals or clinics, yet healing takes place there. We must learn to make our places of worship amenable to healing.
2. Parishioners often do not think of pastors as on a par with physicians and therapists in relationship to healing. There are a variety of ways to make the three visible together and cooperative. It is worthwhile to explore the ways.
3. Preaching the healing stories from Jesus' ministry adds validity to the church's healing ministries, especially when we show that healing is a part of our salvation, not a recent add-on. The early church practiced healing regularly until the Renaissance.
4. Pastors should take time to learn how to do the healing ritual well, and by quoting James 5:13-16.
5. A healing service can be a simple prayer and anointing event or featured in or following a full worship service. It should be done often enough for it to become an expected part of meeting the needs of the congregation.

6. Communication with other clergy, with medical and mental health professionals may take some extra effort. It is usually worthwhile, and sometimes reciprocated.
7. Take time to read the fine recent resources that discuss the theology, the practice, and the future of healing ministries in the church. The selected bibliography at the end of this book lists the best sources.

Membership Vow Renewal

Some congregations are now finding it valuable to the practices of the congregation and to its soul to have a regular schedule of saying the membership vows. These can sometimes be found in the denominational hymnal or worship handbook. Naturally the vows must fit the congregation's soul, the denomination's tradition, and add a cohesive element to the interpersonal relationships among parishioners.

There is little question that when personal participation is added to worship services, the benefits are enhanced. We may assume that membership vows are thus enhanced and strengthened when they are repeated in unison, often enough to be memorable. They are even more effective if the rest of the service features their value.

A caution must be added here. Most vows of membership do not include a promise by participants to obey what elected leaders of the congregation decide on their behalf. This means that in a worst-case scenario, if the congregation finds itself in a court case with an obstreperous parishioner, there is no appeal to these vows. Further, only recently have vows to honor and respect other parishioners been added to membership vows. In the absence of many models of membership vows appropriate to our day, the following are offered:

> LEADER: Do you confess Jesus Christ as your Savior and Lord?
> CONGREGANTS: *I do so confess.*
> L: Do you promise to be his faithful disciple?
> C: *I do so promise.*
> L: Do you commit yourself to be a faithful member of this congregation, through regular attendance at worship, prayer for its mission, love for its members, and sharing of talents and resources?

C: *I commit myself to all of these disciplines.*

L: Will you accept the teachings of the pastor, denomination, and teachers, and if you dissent, follow congregational guidelines for registering your dissent and accepting decisions of elected officials?

C: *I accept such teachings, guidelines, and decisions.*

L: Will you honor our diversity by patient listening and loving responses?

C: *I will learn and express such behavior.*

L: If leading, will you do so respectfully, seeking consensus and God's purposes?

C: *When leading, I will follow these principles.*

L: When you are sick, grieving, in despair, or guilty of sinful misconduct, will you seek spiritual healing, comfort, guidance, and assurance of pardon from spiritual leaders of the congregation?

C: *With thankfulness I will seek such ministries.*

L: Will you share responsibility for making this a joyful, creative congregation?

C: *I will delight in this congregation's celebrations and happiness.*

L: And now, in the living of your vows, may the Lord bless and keep you, may the Lord inspire you in service, and may the Lord grant you peace. Amen.

The Prayer Exchange

The Prayer Exchange, or as it was once called, the intercessory prayer, has highest value to the individual souls and corporate soul of a congregation. This, of course, is the type of prayer that focuses on one person or situation and continues to petition God for a positive response until the supplicant feels confident of God's response. This is different from meditations or healing prayers. And it is a powerful instrument of peace wherever it is practiced.

The Prayer Exchange can take several forms. There can be a regular rotation of names among those who agree to such prayers. There can be random drawing of names for a specified period. There can be a congregationwide round-robin style or it may be limited to a small group. Two individuals may make a commitment for such prayer to each other for any length of time.

There is added value when there are classes offered on prayer and meditation, sermons preached with this reference point with music and sacraments highlighting such prayers in the worship service. Individuals and the whole congregation need not wait for some formal plan or for a high-profile tragedy before engaging in focused, intense prayers. The benefits to all involved souls are well worth this extra discipline. Needless to say, such prayers can focus on a mission field, a politician, an epidemic, war, or great celebrations. "The congregation that prays together, stays together." Even if this is a timeworn aphorism, it is still true.

The Clergy-Killer Phenomenon

The clergy-killer issue is saved to last in this prescriptive chapter, not because it is of least importance, but because there is still so much to say about it. If you are acquainted with my best-selling book by this title, you will not be surprised by what I write here. And if you have not read that book, I encourage you to do so if there is or could be a clergy killer in your life and ministry. While there is no need to repeat, I do want to offer three urgent comments:

1. If you and your elected leaders have not installed the Grievance-Suggestion Procedure (GSP), do so soon. It can literally save your life and the mission of the congregation. GSP works best if installed *before* a clergy killer appears. And even if a clergy killer is active in your congregation, studying and trying to install a GSP can give leaders more confidence in dealing with such a perpetrator. If one is present and active, be assured that he or she and cohorts will try to bypass its process. This is why we encourage the new membership vows in addition to installing a GSP. A board and pastor have more leverage if the clergy killer has already vowed to accept the discipline of these vows.
2. Whether or not you encounter a clergy killer, your very best defense and offense is to keep yourself healthy in body-mind-spirit. When you are uniformly healthy, you will be stronger than the clergy killer, and with God's grace and support from family and others, you can prevail, to the benefit of all. This encouragement to full health of body-mind-spirit does not

imply an attempt to manage a clergy killer conflict alone. Without strong support, a clergy killer will isolate the loner and proceed with the abuse, for clergy killers have no scruples or shame in the methods they use to achieve nefarious ends. This leaves any targeted person who lives by Christian principles, and fights alone, at a mortal disadvantage.

3. When you see or hear of a sister or brother pastor in close encounter with a clergy killer, give all the support you can. Pastors have been trained to be loners, which makes them vulnerable. If there is no local clergy support group, begin one and welcome especially any who struggle with a clergy killer without adequate support. If the early warnings (see the list in the *Clergy Killer* book) appear, do not wait; establish a workable agenda of defense of self and congregation. The earlier healthy strategies to interdict the beginnings of abuse are initiated, the more likely that the conflict can be settled peaceably. If abuses are already underway, prepare carefully for an intervention, whereby strong elected leaders, denominational officials, and wise, prayerful colleagues and parishioners rally in support of justice and peaceable resolution.

Summary

A variety of aids for both sick and healthy congregations are available now. Look for them carefully, for not all that glitters is gold in proffered prescriptions for the ills of congregations. This book offers these Instruments of Peace as prescriptions because they are built on long experience and are compatible with our theology and polities. They also offer specific guidance so you may choose the ones that fit your needs. My prayers accompany your faithful and creative ministries to bring healing and health to troubled congregations and even more empowerment to our normal and paradigmatic congregations.

CHAPTER SEVEN

Pastoral Self-Care and Detoxification

The health of the pastor is crucial to the health of the congregation. The health of the congregation is crucial to the health of the pastor. Like a marriage? Like a codependency? Like a partnership? Like a generative team?

The relationships between pastor and congregation are unique and yet consistent with other organized human groups. Research, consulting observations, and experience indicate this double-natured connection. The uniqueness derives primarily from the reality and illusion that a pastor represents God in some way, leaving laity in an inferior position of spirituality and authority. In this virtual (idealized, imagined) relationship, such uniqueness is ambiguous because each participant has a personal and conditioned expectation for the relationship. Yet, it can be deeply nurturing and generative when enough participants are seeking a disciplined relationship with God. In real-time congregations, however, the relationship can be abused or abusive, and is often distorted, as when there is a conspiracy between pastor and laity to operate the congregation as a small business. This is a common and attractive conspiracy, as has been noted often. Such an agreement often has a contractual nature in which the pastor is "hired" (and fired), the elected board acts as a board of directors, the parishioners are customers, the governing reference point is "the bottom line," and the pastor's job is to keep the board and parishioners happy. We must add, however, that competent business practices have a legitimate place in congregational management, if the dominant agenda is the health of both pastor and congregation, and the soul of the congregation is given full support to generate God-ness (God's generative energy operative).

Though such congregational distortions are a main concern in this book, this chapter is limited to recognizing the two opening premises, then considering the four listed possibilities, followed by prescriptions for the pastor's personal life and for the role of pastor.

What Happens to the Pastor in Toxic Situations

With *toxic congregations*, pastors have a relationship that resembles a marriage. In the country club example, the marriage was something like a serial marriage, followed by a temporary but near fatal infatuation that ended in divorce. In the second toxic example, the marriages between a series of competent pastors occurred through deception in which the Bowlers, needing a pastor to make the congregation appear to be traditional and attractive to newcomers, used misinformation to attract each pastor. Then with the pastor installed, they began their toxic tyranny of pastor and any resistant members, until they left, battered and disillusioned—a piteous divorce in which the conditions causing it were never discussed or remedied publicly nor reported realistically to any pastoral candidates.

The third toxic case resembles a series of bigamous relationships. Each subsequent pastor found himself in bed with two spouses. Each was powerful enough to exact equivalent controls over congregation and pastors. The toxic condition consisted of two toxins that neutralized each other, yet had enough potency to impair, sicken, and finally force each pastor to leave in order to survive.

Observations

1. What happened to the pastor in each case?
2. How did the pastor handle the situation (read between the lines)?
3. What would you prescribe for each pastor (review chapters 5 and 6)?

What Happens to the Pastor in Dysfunctional Situations

With *dysfunctional congregations*, pastors have a relationship that resembles what is commonly called a codependency. In a codependency two flawed parties or groups establish a close relationship in which each knows (consciously or unconsciously) the other party's flaw and agrees to cover or compensate for it. Thereby both parties invest in the other in ways that support each other's flaw by paying the price to allow it to be sustained.

In the first case reported, the pastor had flaws that kept him personally dysfunctional in ways damaging to him and limiting to the congregation. Yet the congregation, though complaining occasionally, kept ignoring or covering for the pastor's flaws. The pastor, even while seeing the internal division, refused to establish protocols that would allow all parties to cooperate and generate spiritual health. Thus both pastor and congregation denied their own and each other's flaws while trying to appear as a traditional congregation. The codependency broke down when the denominational office sent in a consultant who pointed out the potentially fatal flaws and recommended that there be a change of pastors and retraining for the church board. This was done, but the damage was deep and local conditions now preclude making some of the recommended changes that would facilitate healing and health.

In the second dysfunctional case, a narcissistic pastor gained control of a healthy congregation. By then controlling staff, board elections, finances, and by preaching entertaining sermons, he ingratiated himself to significant members, thus maintaining control and limiting both internal health and needed outreach ministries. He was careful to not violate any denominational regulations and thereby disabled any movements to replace him officially. His part of the codependency was to create flaws that supported his controlling behavior. The congregation's part was to pretend that they had a masterful pastor.

The third dysfunctional case features a hidden dysfunction that sets up a continuing series of disruptive complaints that are handled poorly. The codependency exists as the church board and pastor continue to flounder through case after case of complaints that never are resolved. The congregations accept this as normal, since worship services and programs continue to exist, though without passion and creativity. The denominational office is a coconspirator with board and congregation. The pastor is a coconspirator by simply "going through the motions" of pastoring.

The fourth case of dysfunction is the infamous "clergy-killer" case. This is a case full of passion and abuse, but one in which much of the congregation knows little of what is transpiring as a disgruntled member and his wife wage an attack on the pastor that the board is unable to handle. When the denomination is consulted, it submits to the innuendoes and intimidation of the clergy killer. After the pastor and family have been abused for months, the denomination replaces him. The codependencies consist of a pastor unskilled in managing conflict, and a board that is inept in handling spiritual warfare in the form of fanatical abuse and intimidation on one hand, and the denominational office that covers for the perpetrator and pretends the pastor is at fault on the other hand.

Observations

1. What happened to the pastor in each case?
2. How did the pastor handle the situation (read between the lines)?
3. What would you prescribe for each pastor (review chapters 5 and 6)?

What Happens to the Pastor in Normal Situations

The *normal* congregations offer reassuring examples of less than perfect congregations and competent pastors working as partners instead of as competitors or enemies. The first case shows a healthy congregation traumatized by the sexual misconduct of a beloved pastor, and how they literally become their own pastor by using consensus to handle painful issues. They were aided by a wise consulting pastor who supported their discerning efforts. The second case follows a downtown congregation in a deteriorating neighborhood, facing an uncertain future. This healthy congregation, with the aid of an experienced and compassionate pastor, lays plans for reinvigorating its own worship and ministries, then reaches out to the neighborhood with shared plans for community services that restore this neighborhood to health. The third case exemplifies a pastor under attack turning to the church board and training them to resist the attacker's efforts and move the congregation through healing and into spiritual health.

Observations

1. What happens to the pastor in each case?
2. How did the pastor handle the situation (read between the lines)?
3. What would you prescribe for each pastor (review chapters 5 and 6)?

What Happens to the Pastor in Paradigmatic Situations

The *paradigmatic* congregations push us outside the boxes of parochial and traditional thinking into possibilities for thriving with fresh ways to preach and live the gospel. In the first case, a clergy spouse sees a teaching need/opportunity, experiments, and becomes excited about developing a fresh curriculum built around the imagination of children and Bible stories. As the clergy couple expands the possibilities and discusses them with the church council, a full teaching ministry evolves, that eventually involves the whole community. In the second case a tall-steeple, downtown congregation transforms itself from a flourishing country club ministry to one that involves the whole downtown area of the city. This transformation is built on a spiritually sound congregation, ready to follow a gifted and creative pastor into a full outreach ministry based on community needs. The third case is simulated from fragmentary but convincing information about the virtual congregations developing through the Internet, house churches, study groups, and parishioners who attend a real-time church but want something more. The growth of virtual congregations is remarkable and generating not only great interest and numbers but also stimulating established congregations, denominations, and seminaries to rethink the meaning of *congregation* and *mission*. The virtual congregation makes the role of pastor an open-ended calling in which theology, ministries, programs, and tenure are flexible.

Observations

1. What happens to the pastor in each case?
2. How did the pastor handle the situation (read between the lines)?
3. What would you prescribe for each case (review chapters 5 and 6)?

By now you have noted that in this book you have the opportunity to reach into your experiences, your imagination, your soul, and the soul of the congregation for understanding and prescriptions. This book provides basic information; now comes the opportunity to do what is needed most in contemporary pastoring—open yourself to the gift of discernment promised from the Holy Spirit, then compose a creative prescription for healing and growth.

Here is a simple, yet effective model for organizing this process. It is a simple ABC model that helps focus information gathering into a reference format. The full form can be found in appendix E.

A – Awareness
> What do I know about this issue?
> What do I need to know?
> Where can I find needed information?

B – Basics
> What are the basic resources needed and available?

C – Connections
> What connections are needed with persons or organizations?
> What fresh connection do I need with God for this endeavor?
> How can I most effectively connect my soul with this endeavor?

Perspective

From the toxic and dysfunctional cases, there was no polity or workable guidelines available to direct participants through the serious patterns of toxic contamination or dysfunction. And in these cases the pastor was either part of the problem or unaided in any efforts to heal and nurture. This allowed sin and evil to dominate the congregation.

By contrast, in the normal and paradigmatic cases a relatively healthy congregation already existed, along with an appropriate protocol for managing change; and lay leaders prepared to join the pastor in developing fresh and needed ministries and governance. The pastors in these cases were spiritually disciplined, creative, and experienced enough to lead change or find mentoring for further guidance.

The chapter on emotions, ethics of consequences, engrams, culture, and mimesis (the power of imitation) opened our attention to primary issues in why people act like they do. This reminded us that when we analyze congregations and persons, we must look within for patterns of motivation that need healing and nurture, as well as diagnose behavior and make new rules as remedies.

The prescriptive chapter provided Instruments of Peace to remedy most such situations of impairment. And now in this chapter prescriptions are offered specifically focused on pastoral self-care and healthy management of the pastoral role.

Pastoral Self-Care

We now have a variety of books for pastors that offer plans and methods for self-care. Though self-care is becoming an accepted notion, it is apparent as we see ourselves in mirrors, look at our colleagues, observe our behavior, monitor our internal feelings, check on how we use our energy, and monitor carefully the results of our ministries that we have a ways to go in fulfilling the benefits of self-care. At a preconscious level we worry typically about becoming self-centered, arrogant, or narcissistic. This is a healthy concern, except for our ability to rationalize. For example, some pastors think that by paying little attention to personal health they are thereby investing more time and energy in ministry. Yet, it should be apparent that when we do not take time to eat properly, sleep as needed, exercise appropriately, shortchange our primary intimate relationships, and neglect spiritual disciplines, we become less effective in ministry. It is then only a matter of time before we feel the effects of breakdowns in body-mind-spirit. Further, by neglecting appropriate self-care, we miss opportunities to model the healthy self-care so many of our parishioners need.

As an example, examine this list of clergy maladies that are now so common as to be rightly termed a "clergy syndrome."

DEPRESSION
BURNOUT
ROLE CONFUSION
BOUNDARY VIOLATIONS
ADDICTIONS

Each of these maladies is serious enough in itself. Yet when one is present at least one of the other four is operative as well. Don't be deceived into believing that because these maladies are common among clergy we need not be too concerned, for so many afflicted pastors appear to be functioning normally. Because on closer examination during my years of doing therapy with clergy, I found that pastors who know how to fulfill minimal visible expectations can rather easily camouflage all of these maladies. Sooner or later a breakdown occurs or alert parishioners complain. More of us are celebrating and leading in the emergence of the clergy mentoring and retraining movements, for these offer prime opportunities for clergy to seek healing and health before breakdowns occur.

Self-Care Prescriptions

Space limitations do not allow a full discussion of every important subject in congregational management or pastoral care. So as in other chapters, we focus on the most important issues and remedies or factors that seem neglected in other literature. The first item gives us the general biblical-theological foundation for all healing and health issues. Though it is quite general, a careful reading will indicate that its insights are needed for all the healing and health prescriptions in this book.

Rx: Wholeness

The emerging health crusade in the United States is predicated upon learning to observe and feel this body-mind in action as we try to fulfill our healthy functioning and positive potential. This is a significant and positive change from our present typical lifestyles that are oriented toward appetites, fears, addictions, and codependencies.

Organized religion has a great opportunity to join this reformation and its quest for health and then lift our self-sensitivities beyond this new physical-material awareness, even beyond the metaphysical insights that offer cultic visions of universal health, love, and peace. Currently the holistic vision of health seems like the ultimate goal for medicine, psychology, and helpful alternative therapies. The church at its best, however, offers healing, health, and salvation beyond personal health and comfort.

This is not a pretense nor triumphalism on the part of organized religion and its clergy. Rather, it celebrates the realistic wholeness beyond holistic hybrids of traditional medicine, psychology, and metaphysical therapies. For though medicine, for example, speaks and advertises itself as holistic, it still offers only traditional medicine with favored selections from other therapies added on. Religion, of course, has made a similar mistake over the centuries by offering a ritualized or formulized version of salvation that was supposed to not only offer spiritual peace and eternal bliss, but keep us relaxed, confident, joyful, and compassionate.

Now there is a general awakening to our need for the best of modern medicine, the best of psychology, the best of alternative therapies, and the best of spiritual salvation. God has placed all of these great health resources at our disposal and will help us see that there is no true healing and health without the remedies from all four. Further, there is no wholeness without the full range of healing, health, and active vision of salvation for all persons and all of creation. There is more than a semantic difference between *holism* (a useful neologism) and *wholeness*.

Wholeness needs definition here, even though we already have formal descriptions and popular notions about it. We cannot understand self-care with only our own rationalizations, habits, or anxieties to guide us.

For the purposes of this book, and this chapter on the realities of self-care, the following version of wholeness is offered as a set of dynamic principles.

Principle I
Wholeness is functional. That is, it is designed to fulfill God's purposes for God's creation and the best interests for humankind.

Principle II
Wholeness is connectional. It connects us with the chaos of God's generative energy. (Note: quantum physics defines *chaos* as the unpredictable interactions of continuous transformation; *generative* as

the procreative method of achieving transformation; *energy* as the infinite potency of God's power enlivening humankind and all of creation.)

Principle III

Wholeness is corporate. That is, wholeness is systemic and interdependent. No one is truly whole until all are whole and all of creation is whole. Each of us, and each congregation can participate in wholeness as relative, personal health, while working toward universal healing, health, and salvation.

Principle IV

Wholeness is not perfection. Perfection is the great vision and expectation of the reign of God over all of humankind and the earth. Clearly, this goal has not yet been fulfilled. Yet, with this vision and God's Holy Spirit to guide us, we can participate in whatever level of wholeness is possible with our intentions and limitations. This means that wholeness includes our imperfections, our pain, and our sins as working ingredients in our healing and development.

Principle V

Wholeness is transforming. That is, once we have committed ourselves to God's salvation (wholeness), we begin to participate in discernment, openness, and discipleship as a way of living. Our wills, intentions, and actions are oriented now toward God's purposes.

Effective self-care needs wholeness as a reference point. But as we develop the awareness that we are each accountable to God for personal participation in wholeness, and all of us together are accountable for creation's wholeness, we also need some starting points and continuing guidelines. Following are the simplest guidelines that have emerged for self-care in the national crusade for health.

Rx: Guidelines for Health

1. Eat less
2. Exercise more
3. Drink water
4. Think freely
5. Pray high

Authoritative health literature now suggests simply eating less food totally and eating more nutritious foods, rather than trying to live on diets. This literature also suggests much more physical activity, from physical labor to disciplined regular exercise to simply adding vigorous walking on a regular basis. There is a flipside to this exercise recommendation, namely, the need for rest. The research on rest and sleep does not offer a consistent amount applicable to everyone. Some thrive on five to six hours of sleep, some need seven to nine. However, one factor is pertinent for nearly everyone, and that is in the first two to four hours of deep sleep recovery and healing are essentially accomplished. The goal then is to focus on getting those early hours of sleep without disturbance.

The recommendation to drink water not only means we often need more fluid intake, with an emphasis on drinking water rather than processed and flavored drinks.

These first three health guidelines focus on the body. Yet we know that health for the body also brings benefits for the mind and spirit, just as they nurture each other and the body. The general recommendation for improved mental health may be summed up as "think freely." This, of course, does not mean random thinking or that anything we think is healthy and valid for behavior. Rather, it is pointing out the great benefits of thinking new, creative, even complicated thoughts. It also means making a point of learning new information and ways of thinking. And perhaps most important of all, it means being open to new thoughts, new people, new conditions, and new possibilities. The Apostle Paul was one of the earliest Christian writers to urge "positive thinking" (Phil 4:8-9).

The fifth health guideline reminds us that healing and health for the spirit requires that we focus on what is higher, greater, uplifting, and eternal. This is the guideline that includes worship and prayer. Meditation is now a popular term in all spiritual-mental disciplines. Meditation differs from prayer in that it is a free flow of consciousness toward the deepest experiences of God's presence. This is likely the most highly researched spiritual experience of all the spiritual disciplines with consistently high ratings. From monastic practices to yoga to transcendental meditation to biofeedback, all offer deep relaxation, restoration of spiritual energy, and the deep possibility of God's presence and guidance (more later).

These five guidelines for health do not cover all aspects of body-mind-spirit healing and health, of course. Yet with brevity and clarity they give us a strong reference point from which to write our own prescriptions for health. (For full coverage of clergy health issues, consult my book, *Fit to Be a Pastor* [Louisville, Ky.: Westminster John Knox Press, 2000].)

Rx: Self-Observation

The noted baseball catcher and humorist Yogi Berra is reputed to have added this one to his long list of insightful aphorisms, "You can observe a lot by looking." This bit of humor is a reminder of one of the most important prescriptions for self-care. By developing the skill of self-observation and taking time to do this regularly in disciplined ways, we will better understand ourselves. We can then watch ourselves with pleasure as we improve, rather than react with dismay and guilt as we notice unhealthy, counterproductive thinking and behavior.

I find it useful to have a full-length mirror on wheels in my counseling office. It not only makes a strong visual point, it is helpful to clients when we discuss learning to be self-observant, or as one of my psychology professors often says, learning how to "catch yourself in the act of being yourself." So when I find a client having trouble describing himself or herself or noticing a sole significant factor in appearance, I roll the mirror in front of where this person is sitting or standing and ask for full attention on the mirror image. The first reactions are predictable. "Oh, I look awful!" or "I've got to lose some weight!" or "Not too bad, huh!" Then after getting more comfortable, the self-observer capability we all have begins to activate. Sometimes there is long silence; sometimes tears; best of all, sometimes the client begins to talk to herself. Often there is a homework suggestion to talk to your mirror image about significant features of yourself, or certain memories, or a relationship, or coming event. This self-observation process can be helpful as you learn to present your best appearance at professional events; talk to your spouse about sensitive matters; or just work toward becoming your own best friend. The point, of course, is to become comfortable observing yourself and honestly reflect on what you see in yourself.

I also have a simulated medical form that I give to clients who want to write a brief prescription for themselves when they have a flash of insight during these moments. Having such a symbolic piece of paper in a pocket or purse provides opportunity to jot down the insight immediately, lest it be forgotten. And a collection of these prescription forms begins to exhibit a pattern of growth-inducing insights that can lead to significant change.

A significant aspect of self-observation is taking time to think about how we are thinking about what we are thinking about. (This is not a conundrum but a real possibility.) We can give names to the three ways we think, in order to intentionally choose how we think at a particular time. THINK-1 is our normal, automatic way of thinking. THINK-2 is the occasional mental experience of bursts of inspiration or new ideas or ways of understanding a person.

If we want the desirable experience of thinking creatively and being open to fresh information and ideas, we must intentionally shift into THINK-3 (T-3). This is the thinking mode of persons who practice awareness of how they are thinking about what they are thinking about, so that they can then make an intentional shift out of automatic thinking into deeper awareness and effective decision making. Daniel Goleman's book *Emotional Intelligence* (New York: Bantam Books, 1995) has been helpful as I devised this THINK-3 concept.

Learning to do THINK-3 takes practice, of course, for we tend to avoid new and possibly inspirational thinking. Yet THINK-3 becomes more possible and natural when we learn to manage powerful emotions (review "Agendas of Human Behavior" above) and recognize the beneficial and counterproductive possibilities in our decision making. It aids us in blending the cognition of the brain's left hemisphere with the generativeness of the right hemisphere. This T-3 awareness and self-management prepares us to make the mental-spiritual quantum leaps into a spirituality beyond piety and into an empowerment in which we live as God calls us to live every day.

As believers we also have the Holy Spirit's gift of discernment to guide us in T-3. The spiritual discipline of meditation is especially helpful in reaching this third way of thinking and self-observation. It provides free time to monitor our thinking and emotions. This resembles the life-fulfilling state of being some call "enlightenment" and some call serenity. For Christian believers it resembles the state of mind-spirit Jesus had when he rose beyond normal inhibitions, fears, and ambitions of those around him to speak the truth with boldness and model what he taught. Pentecost introduced this experience to the early church. Now we must develop this lifestyle through mental-spiritual disciplines and lifestyles.

This self-observant skill is particularly useful for pastors, who are in the public eye more often than others, and certainly scrutinized more often, especially in sensitive encounters. The skill can be abused, manipulated, and turned into a performance, of course. When it is used honestly, however, few skills are more valuable.

Rx: Energy Management

Appendix B is an energy management exercise. It is a stylized drawing of a full-page outline of a tree. The instructions for its use are printed on the exercise sheet.

After each of the cases described in the early chapters is a set of questions that invite observation and thought. One question is, "How does this congregation generate and use its energy resources?" This question may be confusing or difficult to answer for persons unaccustomed to noticing how energy is generated and used. To understand this question, a shift must be made from Newtonian to quantum physics. We all must do this more now that we are trying to understand spiritual energy, mental energy, and coded energy. The coded energy concept resembles human cells that contain DNA, in which genes contain the formula for producing the whole person.

The old laws of physics many of us grew up with taught us to think of energy as fuel that is burned to produce motion and power. Now we are learning that energy is the stuff that makes up the universe. It can take material form as a chair or human body, or it can remain in its more primal form as the chaotic, generative essence of God's presence. We all have access to this immaterial energy, for it actually is the substance we use to think, move our bodies, and relate to one another. It is present everywhere and each molecule is coded with the design of the whole universe. Actually, we have no truly or fully descriptive word for this expansive understanding of energy. I refer you again to the most helpful book on the quantum sciences I have found: Diarmuid O'Murchu's *Quantum Theology* (New York: Crossroad Publishing, 1997, 39ff.).

The persistent question about energy as a constituent of congregations reveals much about its soul—about its true intentions and its discipleship. The tree exercise in appendix B asks us to do an estimated recollection of where our individual supply of energy goes each day or each week or whichever period you choose to chart. Writing a name of experience on each branch tells one significant use (drain) of the energy available to you personally. Writing a name of experience on each root of the tree tells one significant source of the energy available to you in a given time period. Quantify each experience you have written on the branches and roots with a number from one to ten. Compare the totals for the branches and the totals for the roots to estimate whether you typically operate on an energy surplus or deficit. These total numbers, though only an estimate, provide another indicator of who and what you are by intention and by actual energy use. We know, of course, that though we are each unique in energy use, we each have only a limited amount of energy available in a time period.

If the number totals indicate an energy deficit regularly, burnout is predictable, along with irritability, guilt trips, and the possibility of making big mistakes. A surplus of energy can indicate good health, an unusually efficient agenda, or that you have an unusual amount of energy to invest.

Rx: Ethics of Consequences

This subject has been discussed earlier. It is included here in the personal prescription chapter to remind us that the consequences of human behavior are the most authentic indicators of the meaning of our behavior. No matter what intention we claim or excuse we make, the consequences of personal behavior are a reality check.

Observing and being honest about the consequences of our behavior is a companion skill to being self-observant. An outline of the "Ethics of Consequences" is included in appendix C. A review of this enormously significant shift in global human ethics is important in order for us to incorporate this potent indicator of the effect our thinking and behavior have on others and our environment, as well as ourselves.

Rx: Boundaries

Boundaries have become a kind of code word for clergy that says, "Don't transgress sexual norms in the pastorate." Yet it is also a valuable word for reminding pastors of their finite limits and the value of helping the congregation, as well as the pastor, understand the realistic *role* of pastor.

Sexual vulnerabilities surround the pastoral role. To succumb is tragic. The self-observer process helps us stay aware of our sexuality and need for intimacy. And it offers healthy ways of meeting these needs, avoiding both sexual misconduct and inappropriate possibilities (as in cybersex). The subject of human sexuality (God's gift) and sex (our practice of sexuality) is covered fully in my recent book entitled *Beyond the Scandals* (Minneapolis: Fortress Press, 2003).

Other boundaries are also important. For example, how the pastor lays out daily and weekly schedules; manages pleasure and recreation by engaging in these at appropriate times; establishes routine deadlines for completing necessary tasks; places limits on encounters with persons who cannot control their use of your time; and how she spends money.

Decision making is clearly a necessary skill for setting boundaries. Boundaries are best set by making considered decisions before the boundaries are violated. Other decisions are part of everyday life, and are made by reference to the situation, and the evaluation of possible consequences of choices. The confidence to make necessary decisions readily is a learned skill for many pastors. It becomes easier through self-observation and energy management. Some simple reminders are also helpful when kept in mind for decision-making times. One reminder is to realize that a decision is only a decision, not a judgment for the rest of your life. When we practice good health, we can simply make the best decision we can for each occasion, and trust God, and healthy supporters for the rest. We can also remind ourselves that many decisions can be changed later, or we can make other decisions in support of the first one. Decision making is simple if we let it be and keep ourselves living the spiritual disciplines. Most parishioners want us to be successful, and will help in valuable decisions if we let them.

Rx: Pastoral "Presence"

Ed Friedman (*Generation to Generation* [New York: Guilford Press, 1995]) reintroduced one of the simplest and most effective prescriptions for managing the pastoral role, namely, the nonanxious presence (NAP). In recommending this as a disciplined and practiced resource in personal pastoral care, I frequently take the liberty of adding the "representative" factor to this acronym, such that it becomes nonanxious representative presence (NARP). The nonanxious aspect, as we have been reminded, is effective in calming conflicted, grieving, or didactic situations, besides the benefits for the pastor who has learned to keep herself calm in the midst of turmoil. Yet a pastor offers more than calmness. And when parishioners recognize that a healthy pastor is representing God and the community of faith, they feel reassurance as well as peace.

Most pastors do not have these two characteristics in their physical presence automatically. They must be learned and practiced, not as a manipulation of emotions, but rather because they are a legitimate part of handling conflictual situations. For an experienced, healthy pastor, NARP is part erect posture, part kindly facial expression, and part silence in order to listen to the stressed person. The mirror work mentioned earlier is one way to practice NARP. But inner peace is a spiritual discipline.

Another version of NARP is the "command presence," common to experienced, self-confident, decisive military officers. The differences are who the officer represents and the more aggressive "take charge" attitude that accompanies a tough-minded facial expression. Pastors can use both of these effectively in appropriate situations.

These comments and prescriptions on pastoral self-care and management should not be construed as definitive of pastoral leadership, which is a larger subject. This chapter is intended as assistance for pastors under abusive attack or serving toxic and dysfunctional congregations.

Rx: Persistent Training of Leaders

The frequency of loner-ministry and burnout among pastors are reminders of the enormous value in training lay leaders to share the responsibilities of ministry and administration. The value of trained leaders, especially those elected to make decisions on behalf of the congregation, is readily apparent. Untrained leadership remains one of the most vulnerable aspects of congregational health or sickness. The reasons and excuses are familiar, but the need is now so great as organized religion is being transformed, that we must make the training of lay leaders a very high priority.

The reason I make it a high priority, beyond the well-known reasons, is because elected lay leaders, along with informal leaders, are the keepers of the congregation's soul and have main responsibility for the individual souls of parishioners. This is not a familiar declaration in many religious settings. Remember, the whole concept of soul as the spiritual presence of the congregation and of parishioners' individual souls being part of the corporate soul needs a great deal of exposure and study before it can be welcomed as the *sine qua non* in understanding and managing congregations.

A solid basis for this concept of soul is present though seldom stated in theology, denominational polity, or professional training for pastors. This will, however, be a main theme in the next chapter. It is apparent that what we now regard as training for elected lay leaders is inadequate and offers little training in how to help heal and nurture these souls. And if you read the chapter that gave prescriptions for healing, immunizing, and nurturing congregations, you noted the crucial role of lay leaders in implementing any or all of these prescriptions.

Rx: Mentoring

Having a mentor in pastoral ministry is one of the best prescriptions. Some denominations have established mentoring programs. This works well for some pastors. Yet there is value in having a mentor outside your denominational circles. The important issue is that letting yourself become a loner in pastoral ministry is not only lonely, it can be dangerous. For pastoral ministry is much more complicated now than in past years. Particularly if you are new to pastoral ministry or are having some troubling problems, it is wise to check out the possibilities of seeking a mentor. A mentor can be of great value in supporting a pastor in her self-care, as well as in the *role* of pastor. In other professions, supervision and mentoring are typically required for several years. We have many experienced pastors in our country who have been or can be valuable mentors. Check out the possibilities. When you find one you may have found one of our best prescriptions.

Rx: Don't Do Dumb Stuff

One of the wisest and most appropriate prescriptions I ever heard for pastors as they care for the *role* of pastor came from an experienced woman who was the informal pastor of a tiny mountain valley church. I was a young man accompanying my father as he made his circuit of small mountain congregations that had no pastor. She often spoke in aphorisms, especially to visiting pastors. Before the worship service began, she would make a point of saying to the pastor, "Talk short!" Then in random comments as she was cleaning up the church building after the service, the aphorisms came often. But my favorite was, as is, "Don't do dumb stuff!" If I could only give one word of advice to a young pastor (or any pastor), this would be it. It reminds us how easy it is to make a mistake that comes back to haunt us, or one that injures, or confuses, or betrays a confidence. Here again the value in the skills of self-observation and THINK-3 show their importance. They emphasize the special version of self-awareness in which we can actually monitor our thoughts and intentions *before* they are spoken or done.

CHAPTER EIGHT

Interacting with a Congregation's Soul

Bless the Lord, O my soul;
And all that is within me,
Bless God's holy name!
Bless the Lord, O my soul,
And forget not all God's benefits,
Who forgives all your iniquities,
Who heals all your diseases,
Who redeems your life from darkness,
Who crowns you with steadfast love and mercy,
Who satisfies you with good as long as you live.
Bless the Lord, O my soul;
And all that is within me,
Bless God's holy name. —Psalm 103:1-5 RSV, paraphrased

It was Easter Sunday morning. I had just invited the confirmation class and their sponsors to the chancel. The young people were looking shy. The congregation was beaming.

He was tall and lanky, with craggy, Lincolnesque features and big hands. I recall those hands from our first handshake when his strong, calloused hands engulfed mine in a firm and friendly handshake. And I will long remember those hands as he placed them in blessing on the head of a teenage girl standing in front of him, whom he had mentored through the confirmation classes. I remember also the tears on the cheeks of this sheep farmer as he fulfilled his calling as an elder in the church by confirming her as a member of this community of faith, along with his other deeds of goodwill in the community.

It was Easter Sunday morning at our worship service, the traditional time to confirm as members the young people who had studied to prepare themselves for this occasion. The congregation stood to honor and welcome them. And as I offered the prayer of confirmation, tears of joy were natural. This was the community of faith expressing its soul and welcoming these young, individual souls to participate fully in the corporate soul. There was another presence here.

The woman handing out the confirmation certificates was an elder who served with great competence as stated clerk of this congregation's session. Among her many contributions was the researching and writing of this congregation's history. She read accounts from this history on special occasions and as part of the worship service on Sundays when Holy Communion was observed. Even after the history was written, she continued to solicit personal stories from members of their life in this congregation. And on appropriate occasions (weddings, funerals, etc.) she would read selected portions of the stories with the subject person's permission. She may or may not have meant the word as I use it in this book, but she commented to me that she felt she was helping parishioners understand the soul of this congregation they loved. She read a brief account of a similar Easter in this church at the turn of the century.

Another of the sponsors standing with us in the chancel wore a broad smile as he laid his hands on the teenager in front of him. I had met this remarkable man shortly after arriving at this church in Salem (not the town's true name) as interim pastor. I learned soon that he was the architect of the remarkable teamwork among the elders of this congregation. Though a modest man, he had a benevolent, authoritative presence. Studying and building professional and informal teams for research, special projects, and organization was his area of expertise. As a high official in the Department of Agriculture in Washington, D.C. he traveled the United States helping farmers and agri-businesses organize and do their work most effectively. Though his office was in Washington, his home was in Salem. This produced the long commute he made several times each month in order to worship and serve in this his home congregation. Nearly every time the Session of this congregation met or provided a major church event, he was there. He critiqued and mentored this team of elders very carefully with remarkable results. At every session meeting, whether he was there or not, he had selected and briefed an elder or the pastor to lead a training session, along with the Scripture lesson and silent meditation time.

My conversations with him were stimulating, for we had both studied nearly the same notable authors and consultants in small-group process and leadership. A remark I heard from him frequently was, "Lloyd, in business and political culture we know that team structure, spirit, and performance is crucial to the effectiveness of its organization. Why can't the seminaries, denominational offices, and congregations understand this? So many religious organizations I encounter make little attempt to shape their leadership into caretakers of the organization's mission and competent mentors of all workers they supervise. One of the first things I did when I joined this congregation many years ago was to ask for authority to develop a sense of disciplined pleasure in leadership and mission in this congregation and elected leaders. You see the results."

I asked him if he could state his primary reason for this strategy. He answered thoughtfully, "Because every organization has a soul that is its life force. If that soul is not healthy, the organization will not be either. It takes a team to care for such an important entity. And in my experience, this is true of the church as well as secular organizations." *Soul*—where had he learned this term?

These vignettes are in sharp contrast to the prevalent model seen among so many congregations. The intentions of participants in these boards are often sincere; but the process, agendas, and goals lack appropriate direction, methods, and vision. What are the typical flaws in board meetings? Their goals are unclear or inadequate to the real needs. The direction provided by the moderator, pastor, or committee chairpersons is random and leaves unfinished business. As often as not, such meetings leave participants feeling little meaning in what they have done. There is no soul healing or nurture.

A major share of the blame lies in how congregational leaders are selected, elected, and trained as leaders. They serve because no one else would, or because they felt obligated, or because they wanted to control the board. They have no model for their mission as "soul keepers."

Now that we have seen exemplary board members and presumed the worst about typical boards, let us focus on the themes of this chapter. One theme is to reaffirm that each congregation and congregant has a soul. We have been introducing this theme at every opportunity, for it is the X-Factor in any congregation. The second theme is a plea to regard the elected leaders as the soul keepers of both the corporate and individual souls. The first theme will receive less attention because it has been working throughout the book. Both of these themes apply to the congregations we have been observing. The goal is to make toxic and dysfunctional congregations rarer and normal and paradigmatic congregations prevalent.

Reality check: Most pastors have at least one board member, hopefully more, who functions as well as the ones just described. Yet the conception of a full board serving as soul keepers is best fulfilled when all board members, and pastor/staff, of course, become aware that serving on a soul-keepers board is a much more exciting and worthwhile way to serve God than just attending dull board meetings. The conception of soul keepers is not some strange new faddish idea. But it is revolutionary in its effects and in the empowering of the whole congregation when envisioned and established appropriately. For healthy spiritual relationships are two-way processes. In the soul keepers concept, the board cares for the soul of the congregation, and this soul ministers to the board members. Likewise, as the congregation recognizes that the board cares for the congregation's soul and for the souls of each parishioner, they in turn become supporters of the board. Establishing this way of functioning as a board does not happen overnight or just because it's a good idea. It simply gives a fresh opportunity for pastor, board, and congregation to fulfill their calling.

THEME I: Every Congregation and Parishioner Has a Soul

> For it was you who formed my inward parts;
>   You knit me together in my mother's womb.
> I praise you, for I am fearfully and wonderfully made.
>   Wonderful are your works;
> that I know very well. (Psalm 139:13-14)

Autopoesis. Here's this term from quantum science again that has such notable insights applicable to the soul of an organization (see Margaret Wheatley, *Leadership and the New Science*; Diarmuid O'Murchu, *Quantum Theology*). This is the quality of being in a soul that means it organizes itself internally, adapts to its environment, and has a natural tendency to grow and produce good or evil. No wonder those who try to change an organization often find reactions that are unintended. The application to toxic, dysfunctional, normal, and paradigmatic congregations must be taken seriously.

The secular world appears to have little trouble speaking of the soul of an organization and devising management strategies that treat this soul as a reality (Margaret Wheatley, *Leadership and the New Science*; Stephen R. Covey, *Principle-Centered Leadership*). And noted scientists speak of the soul of the universe as a living reality and individual souls as the emerging multisensory seat of human experience (Fred Alan Wolf, *The Spiritual Universe*; Peter Russell, *From Science to God*; Gary Zukav, *The Seat of the Soul*). Organized religion should not be so slow in discussing its view of soul.

Can speaking of a congregation's soul make any sense in a postmodern, post-Christendom world? It can, if we add more specifically that this is becoming a postmaterialistic age—the age of spirituality. There are no experts in this newest spirituality (not the same as "newer theology"). Almost suddenly nearly all of us are left as pilgrims in a strange land as we venture into the newest awareness of a God much greater ("Mysterium Tremendum"—Rudolf Otto, *The Idea of the Holy*) than the one we try to create in our own image (J. B. Phillips, *Your God Is Too Small*). And a creation that is much more dynamic and generative than we imagined. *Soul* is an "old-new" term that opens fresh thoughts, even though its meaning is nearly the same as *heart* or *spirit*.

In our recent Christian history and presently, we use the word *soul* to represent where God dwells within every human being. But an individual's soul can also be a place where demons dwell and evil lurks. However, even though believers accept the presence of soul, when we use this word to identify a life core in organizations we move beyond popular acceptance and usage.

Carl Jung, the noted Swiss psychoanalyst, identified the soul of an organization as the collective unconscious or an amalgamation of all souls involved in it. Jung's definition is somewhat inadequate. The metaphor that makes the most sense to me and represents the meaning of soul in this book is this metaphor: a single lighted candle represents an individual soul, and a cluster of lighted candles represents the soul of a congregation. The collective soul does not depend on any one candle, yet it includes all who join the group with their candle. Extending this metaphor with the background of Christian history, especially John 1:4, it is the light that represents living spirit. The purer and brighter the light, the more God is present. Each person is a lighted candle and when gathered, together they constitute the brighter collective soul. Yet, I want to add, that the soul of a congregation is greater than the sum of the individual souls, because in the collective, God is manifest in a unique way. In a group of believers, God can generate new possibilities in ways that God cannot with individuals.

Paul suggests that Christ is the head of the church, and we know that he is present when two or more are gathered. This means that God can be present in each individual but also in the collective in a new way. However, this does not mean that God is always present in the gathered. As there can be evil in the soul of an individual, there can be evil in even gathered believers, making these groups toxic. Again, the purer and brighter the light, the more God's grace is manifest. Or as 1 John suggests, love is the character of a group of believers who are reflecting the presence of God. The church without God just becomes another crowd of people.

It is important to think, speak, and act God-ness and soul, especially if God has called us to be spiritual leaders. For with soul as our primary self, instead of body-mind, we can be lifted into a realm of awe, discernment, and joy not possible in our normal lifestyles (cf. Isa 6:1-5, 55:8-9; Acts 10:10-16; 2 Cor 12:2-4; Rev 1:10-19). A powerful kind of spiritual yearning emerges that is not satisfied by a relaxed body or even a creative mind. We are earnestly seeking the highest experiences of God and God-ness in our world that has begun to experience soul, that primal life force that is the other part of us, and fulfills God's reasons for creating us. Soul is not satisfied in business meetings, perfunctory sacraments, wordy worship services, or outreach missions that are self-serving. Soul is satisfied in individual meditative experiences focused on God's presence, in the shared spiritual experiences of the community of faith, and in generating meaning and ministry. One of the tasks of a board composed of soul keepers is to see that not only the administrative necessities of the congregation are taken care of but also that nurture of the soul is primary.

THEME II: The Elected Board Is the Soul-Keeper of the Congregation

> As a deer longs for flowing streams,
>   so my soul longs for you, O God.
> My soul thirsts for God,
>   for the living God. (Psalm 42:1-2a)

Team . . . *Team* . . . TEAM. This is one of the instructive themes in organizational management. The idea of boss, or director, or master has little currency in profitable organizations today. The team concept is replacing hierarchical thinking, yet it is not a perfect model for all groups and organizations.

Teams exist in multiple forms. Independent teams do tasks individually with little dependence on teammates, except for logistics. Project teams are organized and interdependent for specific projects and limited time periods. Virtual teams (sometimes called "Wiki Teams") are suddenly popular, made possible by technology. The Internet allows persons separated by distance, costs, language, and resources to communicate easily, spread workloads, and relate to different environments with the benefits accruing to all participants. An interdependent team works for goals, dependent on each other's skills, energy, ideas, and support.

The elected board of a congregation is an interdependent team, or should be. Interdependence has multiple benefits, yet harbors vulnerabilities. Its characteristics, such as shared information, competition, traditions, shared resources, diversity, personality differences, and group politics can be used positively or negatively. When there is consensus, justice, and respect, the group's synergy can be maximized. When there is misunderstanding, disagreement, favoritism, and inequality, the group flounders. The greater the interdependence, the greater the need for a common vision, clear directions, and satisfying rewards.

A well-trained and disciplined board is in a unique position to become *embedded observers* with the congregation. It becomes privy to most significant information, talents of members, interpersonal relationships, ministry options, as well as the health of the corporate soul. And it has the responsibility, accountability, and authority to act on these factors.

The focus here is on the elected board of the congregation, yet the guidelines and training cues offered here are appropriate for all leaders in the congregation, indeed, eventually for every parishioner. Focusing on the elected board is a natural beginning to whatever group training is used to prepare leaders to become soul keepers, for most denominational polity declares them to be primarily responsible for the welfare of the congregation. My Presbyterian Church (USA) *Book of Order*, the official guide to doctrine and governance in the denomination, gives to the session the responsibility for "the peace, purity, and unity" of the congregation. Other committees, boards, and units of ministry have related responsibilities and are accountable to the board for assigned duties and support of the board and pastor and staff. If it is feasible, training in group process and leadership can be provided at the same time for all, including the pastor. The congregation should be informed, in appropriate ways, that this training is occurring and of its purposes.

Guidelines for Training Congregational Leaders for Their Role as Soul Keepers

1. Soul-keeper training should be done as an official act of the denomination and/or congregation.
2. The materials, methods and exercises used should be appropriate to the congregation's needs and resources.
3. If at all possible, an appropriately trained consultant should be engaged to do the training for the first tier trainees—pastor, staff, moderator.
4. Group process and leadership training, and in particular the SK training, should begin with at least a two-day intensive training period, preferably a full week, with regularly scheduled continuing education.
5. If circumstances limit the training, shortened or sequential training processes can be used, such as:
   A. Training the pastor/staff to train others
   B. Concentrating the training on one segment of the training at a time
6. Reviews, mentoring, and evaluations are a necessary part of the training.

The Training Format for Soul Keepers

1. Individual preparation for soul keeper training:
   A. Personal, prayerful dedication to complete the training
   B. Fill out the "Reflecting on Your Own Spiritual Health" form (appendix F)
   C. Write out your reasons for: (1) joining this congregation; (2) agreeing to stand for election to the board; (3) completing the soul keeper training

D. Discuss this training project fully with your spouse and family, and attempt to gain their support

E. Begin to intensify your personal commitment to healing and health (see earlier prescription for a healthier lifestyle)

F. Fulfill all preparation projects required for the training

2. Board preparation for soul keeper training:

A. Notify denominational office of this training commitment

B. Arrange appropriate financial and accountability factors involved

3. Congregational preparation for soul-keeper training:

A. Prayerful support

B. Adjusting to changes required during and after this training

Components of the Soul Keepers Training

1. Do the required preparation projects
2. Study and practice the self-care prescriptions discussed in chapter 7
3. Carefully study the evidence of the soul of this congregation
4. Find and study the official or informal history of this congregation. If there is none, arrange a congregational process of small groups to compile records and write such a history.
5. Study chapter 5, "Why People Act Like They Do"
6. Study chapter 6, "Instruments of Peace"
7. If you are clergy or staff, study chapter 7, "Pastoral Self-Care and Detoxification"
8. Study group process and leadership materials
9. Study the healing, health, and nurture of the soul of this congregation
10. Begin preparations for small-group classes to train the congregation in the awareness and care of their personal soul, and the corporate soul
11. Study the role of embedded observer in the congregation— the process of watching for signals of spiritual growth and spiritual sickness
12. Lay plans for the short-term and long-term mission of this congregation

Note: My colleagues and I can offer seminars on all or parts of the material presented in this book. Also recommended as one of the best sources for such training is The Alban Institute, 2121 Cooperative Way, Suite 100, Herndon, VA 20171.

Summary

The introduction laid out a plan and definitions for the study of the truly sick congregations in the United States, compared with those more healthy and paradigmatic. Cases illustrating four types of congregations were offered to indicate these conditions. The causes of human behavior, both good and bad, was presented to aid in understanding how congregations become toxic or dysfunctional, and why others are healthy and creative. The Instruments of Peace chapter laid out prescriptions for healing, immunization, and health in congregations. Special attention was paid to pastoral self-care in chapter 7. And the final chapter offered rudiments of leadership training designed to discover, heal, and nurture the soul of the congregation, and those of parishioners.

This book is designed as a primer in identifying and treating sickness and health in congregations by using standard prescriptions and nurturing procedures. And it added a significant fresh factor through understanding the soul of organizations and individuals. This soul factor is strange to those not acquainted with the newer insights from the management and leadership fields and the quantum sciences. The sincere belief undergirding this soul factor is that it opens communities of faith to the transformational spirituality emerging through the work of God's Holy Spirit in our day. Global forms of this newer spirituality are developing outside organized Christianity. This book then joins many others in attempting to urge and guide Christianity to help lead this remarkable global awareness.

Since this book is designed as a primer and textbook, the coverage of the several themes and programs is brief. The selected bibliography offers supplementary material. Primers and textbooks are intended to start thoughtful persons on a new pilgrimage. That is my prayer for this book.

The new work of art does not consist of making a living or producing an objet d'art or in self-therapy, but in finding a new soul. The new era is the era of spiritual creativity . . . and soul-making.
—Henry Miller

BMS FITNESS OUTLINE

Daily -Weekly Regimen

BODY

- Stretching, flexing movements (in early morning or midday or evening).
- One aerobic exercise 5 days/wk (warm up before strenuous exercise; do 15–20 minutes per session).
- Eat less (if you can do so safely, cut your food consumption in half).
- Eat wisely (follow Food Guide Pyramid; savor, be thankful).

MIND

- Prepare brief and realistic schedule for the day.
- Do brief mental relaxation exercises throughout the day (stretch slowly, especially shoulders, neck, arms; breathe deeply and slowly).
- Practice simplicity (keep lifestyle and decision making simple and relaxed).
- Explore new and old ideas and activities.
- Keep a positive and open attitude.

SPIRIT

- Enjoy being your creative, active self.
- Develop a positive meditative exercise (in early morning or midday or evening).
- Do union-communion prayers throughout the day (savor relationships with God, persons, ecology).

ENERGY MANAGEMENT INVENTORY

The tree is a metaphor for management of personal energy resources. It is a living organism with a number of characteristics: (1) It has root and leaf systems that generate energy effectively. (2) Energy IN must equal energy OUT. (3) The size and contribution of the tree depend upon the health of its life-support abilities and environment. (4) The tree is part of an ecological system and cannot exist in isolation. All of our daily relationships (family, professional, and so forth) drain or restore energy. When energy systems change, the tree must adapt. Energy exists in various forms and potential. The physical, intellectual, emotional, and spiritual apparatus that derives our personal energy is limited. It cannot derive energy without resources and systemic health. Because the environment and the system change over time, the ability to adapt is crucial. Any change—good as well as bad—uses energy. Crises and persistent stress not only use energy, they strain and may damage the energy system. Paying attention to the management of our energy system is not selfish; *it is good stewardship.* Notice that some tasks and relationships both enhance and drain energy.

EXERCISE #1
Use the branches in the illustration on the facing page to list all the tasks and relationships that require energy from you. Then quantify (from 1 to 10) the energy drain of each. Add the total and record it.

EXERCISE #2
Use the roots to list energy intake from other sources. Then quantify each (from 1 to 10). Record the total and compare it to the total in Exercise #1.

EXERCISE #3
List unusual energy drainers or enhancers in your life this week, quantify them, and add to the totals in #1 and #2. Is there an energy deficit? What will balance the totals?

EXERCISE #4
Describe your philosophy for managing your individual energy system.

(Use the blank paper at the end of this book for your comments on these issues.)

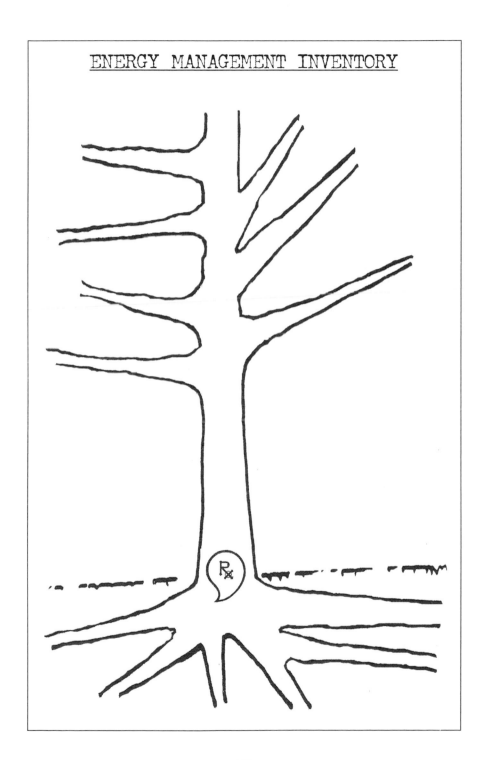

COMPARISON OF ABSOLUTIST AND CONSEQUENTIAL ETHICS

ABSOLUTIST ETHICS

1. Truth is absolute.

2. Truth can be known.

3. Truth is universally applicable.

4. Behavior that violates truth is unethical.

5. Ethical behavior benefits all.

CONSEQUENTIAL ETHICS

1. There are no absolutes, only consequences.

2. Behavior has shared, cumulative consequences.

3. The mind is the reference point.

4. Decision making is the ultimate behavior.

5. Negotiation is the primary skill.

6. *Fairness* is morality.

7. Learning is experiential.

8. Research on consequences is key to the future.

9. We know God and one another through consequences.

10. Beliefs and values emerge from consequences.

CONFLICT OVER HEALING: A CASE STUDY

The pastor began raising the issue of healing about a year after he came to the congregation of 340 members in a medium sized town. First, he told the church board (vestry, session, deacons, etc.) that he believed this congregation, and every congregation, should have regular healing services. His rationale was:

1. Healing is a natural, biblical part of ministry.
2. Healing has become totally secularized in the United States.
3. Healing is needed by some parishioners now, and all of us sometimes.
4. This congregation's healing services should be simple, interactive, and consist of Scripture, music, testimonials, silence, and prayers, with other ingredients possible as needed.
5. The services should be led jointly by the pastor and a layperson.

The board had several lively discussions of this possibility. There was disagreement about whether or not to do this, and how to do it. By official vote, the board decided to mail a letter to the congregation asking if each member wanted such a service, and if so, what kind of service would be appropriate.

About 45% of the respondents wanted such a service; 32% did not; 23% were ambivalent. And there was a wide range of suggestions about content.

The board, by a small majority, voted to have one healing service as a test of use. It was announced to the congregation in usual ways. Sixteen people attended and were enthusiastic about continuing. But a small group of dissidents had been expressing strong opposition to healing services. They said such services were an embarrassment and made their congregation appear too full of sick persons; that "charismatics" would take over their church; and that the pastor was beginning to get "too quirky."

The opposition group was led by a prominent physician and his extended family who had been members for many years. They all indicated that they would stop paying their pledges if there were any more healing services.

REFLECTION AND DISCUSSION
Reread this case and underline significant issues.
1. What are the healthy aspects of this case?
2. What are the dangers?
3. What are your suggestions for managing this conflict?

ABC'S WORKSHEET

ABC's is a familiar designation for essentials, and a useful organizing acronym. Keep it simple.

A – AWARENESS = Conscious, Focused Attention
"What do I know, and need to know
about_____?"

1.
2.
3.

B – BASICS = Primary Ingredients
"What do I have, and need to have?"

1.
2.
3.
4.
5.

C – CONGRUENCY = Interactive Connections
"What are the primary relationships I have and need?"

1.
2.
3.

What do these ABC's tell me?

REFLECTING ON
YOUR OWN SPIRITUAL HEALTH

EXERCISE I: It is healthy to do periodic spiritual checkups, alone, and with a spiritual guide or spiritual friend. Following are two ways to do this.

On the Spiritual Lifeline, place dots in chronological sequence, representing key events that influenced your spirituality, above and below the straight line connecting birth and now. This straight line represents your normal spiritual state. Above the line indicates positive experiences. Below the line indicates negative experiences. How far above and below indicates the intensity of each experience. Number the dots and identify the experience each dot represents at the corresponding number on the Experience Identification list. Connect the dots with a line. Notice trends.

SPIRITUAL LIFELINE

BIRTH   NOW
. . . / _____ / . . .

EXPERIENCE IDENTIFICATION LIST:

1.   5.
2.   6.
3.   7.
4.   8.

EXERCISE II: Reflecting on your spiritual definitions indicates both your beliefs and, by implication, the deviations between your beliefs and your behavior. Think through your definitions carefully, and let them speak to your everyday behavior.

1. Spirituality is
2. Loving is
3. Sin is
4. Transformation is
5. God's purposes are
6. Our congregation's spiritual health is

Glossary

The following terms are offered in definition form as a study aid to this book. These definitions may differ from those of the dictionary or certain authors, but they indicate the meanings they hold in this book.

ABSOLUTIST ETHICS – A type of ethical system that holds these beliefs: truth is absolute; truth can be known; this truth is universally applicable; behavior that violates this truth is unethical; ethical behavior based on this truth benefits everyone.

AUTOPOESIS – From the quantum sciences comes this name for a living entity (soul) at the core of any system. It literally creates itself out of interaction with other entities. Then it impels itself to survive, to adapt to the environment, and to be generative of whatever serves its purposes.

CHAOS – Quantum chaos theory has replaced the Newtonian idea that chaos is disorder, confusion, and anarchy. Instead, chaos now refers to the continuous global swirl of energy and interacting entities that reproduce themselves and may transform themselves into complex forms that are not predictable, yet are dependable. The awareness of this enormous, interactive energy is so complex that even scientists can only try to describe it rather than define it.

CONGREGATION – From the many definitions of *congregation*, this book suggests that a congregation is a persistent gathering of persons to worship, study relevant themes, minister to human needs, and nurture the emergent soul of this group. All the traditional definitions were based on a physically present group of persons—the real-time congregation.

With the emergence of the "virtual" congregations (Internet), we must now open the definition to something like this: "The intentional, physical or nonphysical gathering of persons for religious purposes."

CONSEQUENTIAL ETHICS – This is an emerging ethics derived from earlier pragmatist ethics and the contemporary sense of entitlement and distrust of authority. As opposed to Absolutist Ethics, it believes the only absolutes are the consequences of human behavior, and these consequences are shared and cumulative, thus making consequences an realistic reference point. It forces everyone to take into account the effects of their behavior on other persons, while dealing with the effects of the behavior of others on themselves.

ENERGY – Once thought to be power to make things happen, quantum physics now teaches that energy is the stuff of the universe. According to Einstein's formula for energy, physical mass and energy are identical in that everything is made of energy. For Christians the new definition of energy essentially describes "God-ness," meaning energy is the spiritual essence of a generative God.

ENGRAMS – A theoretical construct explaining how we build and retain distinct memories and definitions of experiences, objects, and pertinent details of something important to us. We form a mental image of presumptions that, for us, becomes all we need to know about what we are defining. It is permanent unless strong contradictory information is encountered.

EVIL – This term has various meanings and manifestations in popular and theological usage. Here it is a generic term referring to a spiritual presence opposed to God and godly purposes. It may produce a lifelong or temporary orientation for some persons, resulting in sinful patterns of living, or as conscious or unconscious acts of sin harmful to others or God's creation.

GOD-NESS – A concept more than a word, it refers to the essence of God, present to us as unusual experiences of love, grace, and experiences of the sacredness in creation, other persons, or ourselves. It is intended to keep God in our experience as "Mysterium Tremendum" (Rudolf Otto).

GOODNESS – This is not the opposite of evil, but corresponds to sin as a choice(s) to participate in evil. Goodness is a culture of high morality when lived by many, and a choice to participate in God-ness by individuals.

QUANTUM SCIENCE – Used here this is a generic term that separates contemporary science from Newtonian science. Physics, chemistry, mathematics, and astronomy are the primary originators and definers of this science of dynamic, interactive participation of all creation in the infinite dimensions of reality and generativity, such that the whole of anything is greater than the sum of its parts, and energy in its various forms is the X-Factor generating, uniting, and moving all things. In popular usage, *quantum* means a quantitative move ahead, that something is much bigger than we imagined.

SOUL – In theological terms the human soul is our individual portion of God-ness—some say it is the *Imago Dei*, God's copyright imprinted on human beings at creation. Soul is not visible, tangible, nor destructible. Yet it is an integral part of the body-mind-spirit (soul) that composes a human being. It is volitional in that this spiritual presence forms us, even as we form it.

SPIRITUALITY – Basically this popularized term simply means immaterial and related to God. In a theological sense it means related to the realms of spirit, and may be oriented toward goodness or evil. Our more common usage refers to levels of morality, and the quality of life most representative of God.

TOXIC – Poisonous, contaminating, impairing, and noxious in the normal physical sense. In this book it means any person, behavior, or established agenda that causes toxic reactions such as physical harm, intimidation, self-serving behavior to the level of evil, and permanent distortion of God's purposes.

VIRTUAL – A relatively new concept related to imagination, time-free, nonphysical activities, and imitating reality and real-time activities. Presently it takes its most popular meanings from Internet activities and potentialities. As used in this book it refers to forms of congregational behavior, without physical presence, unrelated to traditional religious denominations, and driven by the Internet communications between persons united temporarily or long-term by consensual religious beliefs and activities.

Selected Bibliography

Ammerman, Nancy T., ed. 1998. *Studying Congregations: A New Handbook.* Nashville: Abingdon Press.

Becker, Penny Edgell. 1999. *Congregations in Conflict: Cultural Models of Local Religious Life.* New York: Cambridge University Press.

Careago, Andrew. 2001. *eMinistry: Connecting with the Net Generation.* Grand Rapids: Kregel Publications.

Chaves, Mark. 2004. *Congregations in America.* Cambridge, Mass.: Harvard University Press.

Dossey, Larry. 1996. *Prayer Is Good Medicine.* San Francisco: HarperSanFrancisco.

Dudley, Carl S. 2003. *Effective Small Churches in the Twenty-first Century.* Nashville: Abingdon Press.

Eden, Donna. 1998. *Energy Medicine.* New York: Penguin Putnam.

Evans, Abigail Rian. 1999. *The Healing Church: Practical Programs for Health Ministries.* Cleveland: United Church Press.

Foster, Richard J. 1978. *Celebration of Discipline: The Path to Spiritual Growth.* San Francisco: Harper & Row.

Fox, Matthew. 1988. *The Coming of the Cosmic Christ.* San Francisco: Harper & Row.

Frank, Thomas Edward. 2000. *The Soul of the Congregation: An Invitation to Congregational Reflection.* Nashville: Abingdon Press.

Hopewell, James F. 1987. *Congregation, Stories and Structures.* Philadelphia: Fortress Press.

Melander, Rochelle, and Eppley Harold. 2002. *The Spiritual Leader's Guide to Self-Care.* Herndon, Va.: Alban Institute.

Moore, Thomas. 1992. *Care of the Soul: A Guide for Cultivating Depth and Sacredness in Everyday Life.* New York: HarperCollins.

Neuhauser, Peg, et al. 2000. *Culture.com: Building Corporate Culture in the Connected Workplace.* Toronto: John Wiley and Sons Canada.

Olsen, Charles M. 1995. *Transforming Church Boards into Communities of Spiritual Leaders.* Washington, D.C.: Alban Institute.

O'Murchu, Diarmuid. 1997. *Quantum Theology*. New York: Crossroad Publishing.

Polkinghorne, J. C. 1984. *The Quantum World*. Princeton, N.J.: Princeton University Press.

Ratey, John J. 2001. *A User's Guide to the Brain*. New York: Vintage Books.

Rediger, G. Lloyd. 2003. *Beyond the Scandals: A Guide to Healthy Sexuality for Clergy*. Minneapolis: Fortress Press.

———. 1997. *Clergy Killers: Guidance for Pastors and Congregations under Attack*. Louisville: Westminster John Knox Press.

———. 2000. *Fit to Be a Pastor: A Call to Physical, Mental, and Spiritual Fitness*. Louisville, Ky.: Westminster John Knox Press.

Rheingold, Howard. 1993. *The Virtual Community: Homesteading on the Electronic Frontier*. Reading, Mass.: Addison-Wesley.

Robinson, Anthony B. 2003. *Transforming Congregational Culture*. Grand Rapids: William B. Eerdmans.

Schein, Edgar H. 1992. *Organizational Culture and Leadership*, 2nd ed. San Francisco: Jossey-Bass.

Seigel, Daniel J. 1999. *The Developing Mind*. New York: Guilford Press.

Senge, Peter M. 1990. *The Fifth Discipline: The Art and Practice of the Learning Organization*. New York: Doubleday/Currency.

Sisk, Ronald D. 2005. *The Competent Pastor: Skills and Self-Knowledge for Serving Well*. Herndon, Va.: Alban Institute.

Southern, Richard, and Robert Norton. 2001. *Cracking Your Congregation's Code: Mapping Your Spiritual DNA to Create Your Future*. San Francisco: Jossey-Bass.

Wheatley, Margaret J. 1999. *Leadership and the New Science: Discovering Order in a Chaotic World*. San Francisco: Berrett-Koehler.

Wink, Walter. 1998. *The Powers That Be: Theology for a New Millennium*. New York: Doubleday.

Biographical Sketch

G. Lloyd Rediger

Author of seven books on spiritual leadership issues, conference speaker, columnist, pastoral counselor to clergy and their families, consultant, and mentor, Lloyd Rediger has served as pastor, denominational official, legal expert witness, and Senior Trainer for Air Force Command Chaplains. He is married to Vera Hansen Rediger, and lives in Albuquerque, New Mexico.

Index